Publications of the

CENTRE FOR REFORMATION AND RENAISSANCE STUDIES

GENERAL EDITOR   William R. Bowen

ASSOCIATE EDITOR   Joseph Black

Renaissance and Reformation Texts in Translation, 6

SERIES EDITOR   Erika Rummel

Victoria University

in the

University of Toronto

Whether
Secular Government
Has the Right to
Wield the Sword
in
Matters of Faith

A Controversy in Nürnberg in 1530 over
Freedom of Worship and the Authority of
Secular Government in Spiritual Matters

Five Documents

Translated, with an Introduction and Notes, by

James M. Estes

Toronto

Centre for Reformation and Renaissance Studies

1994

CRRS Publications
Centre for Reformation and Renaissance Studies
Victoria University in the University of Toronto
Toronto, Canada M5S 1K7

Canadian Cataloguing in Publication Data

Main entry under title:

Whether secular government has the right to wield
 the sword in matters of faith : a controversy
 in Nurnberg in 1530 over freedom of worship and
 the authority of secular government in spiritual
 matters : five documents

(Renaissance and Reformation texts in translation ; 6)
Includes bibliographical references.
ISBN 0–9697512–4–9

1. Freedom of religion – Germany – Nuremberg –
History – 16th century – Sources. 2. Religion and
state – Germany – Nuremberg – History – 16th century –
Sources. 3. Reformation – Germany – Nuremberg –
Sources. 4. Nuremberg (Germany) – Church history –
16th century – Sources. I. Estes, James Martin,
1934–   . II. Victoria University (Toronto, Ont.).
Centre for Reformation and Renaissance Studies.
III. Series.

BR359.N8W54 1994   261.7′2′094332   C95–930140–2

Cover illustration: woodcut of Nürnberg, from the *Liber chronicarum* (1493).
Reproduced with permission from the copy in the Thomas Fisher Rare Book
Library, University of Toronto.

Contents

Abbreviations

AE	Martin Luther. *Luther's Works*. Ed. Jaroslav Pelikan and Helmut T. Lehmann. Philadelphia: Fortress Press, 1955ff.
Brecht, "Gutachten"	Martin Brecht. "Ob ein weltlich Oberkait Recht habe, in des Glaubens Sachen mit dem Schwert zu handeln: Ein unbekanntes Nürnberger Gutachten zur Frage der Toleranz aus dem Jahre 1530." *Archiv für Reformationsgeschichte* 60 (1969):65–75.
Brenz, *Frühschriften 2*	Johannes Brenz. *Werke, Eine Studienausgabe. Frühschriften, Teil 2.* Ed. Martin Brecht, Gerhard Schäfer, and Frieda Wolf. Tübingen: J.C.B. Mohr (Paul Siebeck), 1974.
Estes, *Christian Magistrate*	James M. Estes. *Christian Magistrate and State Church: The Reforming Career of Johannes Brenz.* Toronto: Univ. of Toronto Press, 1982.
Osiander, *Gesamtausgabe 3*	Andreas Osiander d. Ä. *Gesamtausgabe.* Vol. 3, *Schriften und Briefe 1528 bis April 1530.* Ed. Gerhard Müller and Gottfried Seebaß. Gütersloh: Gerd Mohn, 1979.
Schmid	Hans-Dieter Schmid. *Täufertum und Obrigkeit in Nürnberg.* Schriftenreihe des Stadtarchivs Nürnberg, vol. 10. Nürnberg, 1972.
Seebaß	Gottfried Seebaß. *"An sint persequendi haeretici?* Die Stellung des Johannes Brenz zur Verfolgung und Bestrafung der Täufer." *Blätter für Württembergische Kirchengeschichte* 70 (1970):40–99.

WA

Martin Luther. *D. Martin Luthers Werke, Kritische Gesamtausgabe: [Schriften]*. Weimar: Hermann Böhlau, 1883ff.

WA–Br

Martin Luther. *Dr. Martin Luthers Werke, Kritische Gesamtausgabe: Briefwechsel*. Weimar: Hermann Böhlau, 1930ff.

WA–DB

Martin Luther. *Dr. Martin Luthers Werke, Kritische Gesamtausgabe: Die deutsche Bibel*. Weimar: Hermann Böhlau, 1906ff.

Introduction

The Controversy

In the free imperial city of Nürnberg, which was a major centre of
German economic and cultural life, Luther's message first took root
in 1517 in the humanist circle whose small but socially prominent
membership cultivated close relations with the local Augustinian
monastery. Soon, however, the message spread to the larger
community. By 1522 the city's most important clergymen were all
young Lutherans. By the end of 1524 the great majority of the
population as well as the majority of the city council were
supporters of the Reformation. In 1525 the council removed
Nürnberg from the jurisdiction of the Catholic hierarchy and, acting
on the advice of the city's preachers, assumed responsibility for
establishing the Reformation in the city. In 1528 Catholic teaching
and ceremonies were formally abolished in the city and its subject
territory and replaced by Lutheran doctrine and worship. By 1530
the first steps had already been taken that would culminate in 1533
in the joint proclamation by Nürnberg and the neighbouring
principality of Brandenburg-Ansbach of a church ordinance
(*Kirchenordnung*), that is, a law prescribing uniform doctrines and
ceremonies for the churches in the two territories. Moreover, the
city council, supported by the preachers and true to contemporary
conceptions of government, enforced compliance with its new
ecclesiastical order and would not tolerate Anabaptists or any other
religious dissidents.[1] When, in the spring of 1530, a prominent
citizen raised his voice against this policy of enforced orthodoxy

---

[1] For a good brief introduction to the history of the Reformation in Nürnberg,
see Gottfried Seebaß, "The Reformation in Nürnberg," in *The Social History of
the Reformation*, ed. Lawrence P. Buck and Jonathan W. Zophy (Columbus,
Ohio: Ohio State UP, 1972), 17–40.

and made a skilfully argued plea for religious freedom, he provoked a brief controversy in which three theologians wrote learned defences of intolerance and in the process explored the whole fundamental question of the authority of secular government in matters of religion. The documents presented here are the principal historical remnants of that controversy.

The controversy in Nürnberg is best understood against the background of general developments in the history of the German Reformation. During the 1520s, the religious situation in most communities that had embraced the Reformation was still too fluid to permit the establishment and enforcement of a rigorous Protestant orthodoxy. Thus individuals who did not otherwise disturb the peace had a certain latitude to believe as they wished. By 1530, however, the Protestant princes and city councils under whose aegis the Reformation had been introduced in the 1520s had begun the process of imposing strict uniformity of doctrine and worship in their territories. These efforts at what historians call "confessionalization,"[2] which continued throughout the 1530s and beyond, frequently provoked vocal opposition to magisterial authority in matters of faith from spokesmen for minorities (Catholic, Lutheran, Zwinglian, or Radical) that felt threatened by the impending orthodoxy. Although much research remains to be done on this subject, it appears that this opposition was liveliest in certain imperial cities. In the period 1533–36, for example, there were in Strassburg and Augsburg controversies analogous to that in Nürnberg in 1530, with broadly similar arguments used on both sides. The Strassburg reformer, Martin Bucer, who was involved in the disputes in both Strassburg and Augsburg, wrote his *Dialogi* (1535) and several other works in defence of magisterial authority over the public exercise of religion as a result.[3]

----

[2] The doctrines to be adhered to were often codified in formal confessions of faith, hence the name "confessionalization." The most famous of these confessions, though by no means the first or the only one, was the so-called Augsburg Confession, which was read before the emperor at the Diet of Augsburg in 1530 and soon accepted as the principal standard of orthodoxy in the Lutheran churches.

[3] See Martin Bucer, *Martin Bucers Deutsche Schriften*, ed. Robert Stupperich et al. (Gütersloh: Gerd Mohn, 1960ff.), 5:432–501, 512–26; 6/2:17–188.

The somewhat earlier controversy in Nürnberg, by contrast, produced no work that was published at the time. Moreover, we are less well informed about the Nürnberg controversy than we are about its counterparts in Augsburg and Strassburg. As a consequence, it is necessary to deal at somewhat tiring length with the complicated question of the provenance and authorship of the documents in this volume before one can discuss their content and significance.

For reasons that will be explained presently, the documents have survived as a complex of manuscript copies in the Municipal Archive at Schwäbisch Hall, the city whose reformer, Johannes Brenz, was an external participant in the controversy in Nürnberg. It was the Brenz scholar Martin Brecht who in 1969 called this complex to the attention of scholars and made the first attempt to establish the authorship of the individual items and to clarify their relationship to one another.[4] Since then the complex has attracted considerable scholarly attention[5] and all the documents have been published in reliable critical editions.[6]

The identity of the man whose views sparked the controversy in Nürnberg remains an open question.[7] All we know for sure is that he was a personal friend and confidant of Lazarus Spengler, secretary of the city council and prominent lay leader of the Reformation in Nürnberg;[8] that he was a supporter of the Reformation;[9] and that he was a well educated man with an impressive

---

[4] Brecht, "Gutachten," 65–67.

[5] Chiefly from Seebaß, Schmid, and from Hans-Ulrich Hofmann in Osiander, *Gesamtausgabe 3.*

[6] Details in notes 38, 39, 44, 46, 47.

[7] Seebaß, 60, has argued that the most likely author was the jurist Johann Hepstein, but neither this nor any of the earlier learned guesses can be sufficiently documented from the extant sources; see Schmid, 276–78.

[8] In Document No. 1 Spengler describes him as "an upright man" who is "like a brother to me." See p. 37.

[9] In a letter of 17 March to Veit Dietrich in Wittenberg (cf. p. 14), Spengler reports that those who have fallen into the "new error" are "not fanatics but good Christians." Moreover, in his memorandum (Document No. 2), the anonymous author addresses himself only to Protestant governments and speaks of Protestants as adherents of the true faith while referring to Catholics and Anabaptists as false believers.

knowledge of the Bible.[10] From this one can deduce that he was either an educated Nürnberg patrician or a member of one of the learned professions (i.e., a lawyer or a physician), the only sort of people with whom Spengler normally had close contact. Evidently disturbed by the refusal of his own government and of others, both Protestant and Catholic, to tolerate Anabaptists,[11] Spengler's friend took the view that secular governments have no authority whatever in matters of faith and that they must tolerate Anabaptists, Jews, or any other religious dissidents whose conduct is orderly and peaceful. Sometime before 17 March 1530,[12] he committed his views to paper, citing both scripture and early works of Luther to good effect in the process, and presented the resulting memorandum (Document No. 2) to Spengler, whose considerable influence with the city council would have been known to him.

Spengler, who made himself a set of notes[13] on the memorandum, instantly perceived that his friend's arguments, if they gained acceptance, would have dramatic and unacceptable consequences. If God's word forbids governments to seek unity of faith and worship among their subjects by taking action against the teaching and worship of dissident groups who remain peaceful, then the city council of Nürnberg and other Protestant governments that

---

[10] See Document No. 2, passim.

[11] See the opening paragraph of Document No. 2, p. 41. The Anabaptist movement gained a foothold in Nürnberg's rural territory as early as the summer of 1526 as a result of the missionary labours of Hans Hut. Only in 1529 did the movement establish itself inside the city walls. Even though the Anabaptists never became numerous in Nürnberg and never constituted a threat to the ecclesiastical or political status quo, the city council, for the reasons elaborated and defended in the documents here translated, took punitive action against them from the beginning. See Schmid, 6–230. The immediate occasion of the anonymous author's concern may have been the difficulties that the city council was having with the obstinate Anabaptist preacher, Bartholomäus Friedrich, who had been in jail since 1528, refused to recant, and had launched a hunger-strike in March 1530. See Seebaß, 58–59; Osiander, *Gesamtausgabe* 3:632.

[12] The date of Spengler's letter to Veit Dietrich (see p. 14 and note 17), which includes the first surviving reference to the anonymous author's views.

[13] Summary and analysis in Osiander, *Gesamtausgabe* 3:633 and Schmid, 287–88.

had expelled the Catholic clergy, abolished mass, and instituted reformed doctrine and worship would have to readmit the banished priests and monks, allow them to teach freely, and permit anyone who chose to do so to take part in all their "godless" and "idolatrous" ceremonies. In other words, the arguments of the anonymous memorandist called into question the basic assumption on which the Protestant reformers and their governmental allies had worked during the 1520s in establishing the Reformation, namely, the conviction that the Christian magistrate has the *cura religionis* (literally, "the administration of religion"), i.e., the divinely imposed obligation to establish true doctrine and worship among his subjects and to abolish false doctrine and worship. Having inherited this conviction from the pre-Reformation period,[14] the reformers had tended simply to assume its truth. Now, in the 1530s, hostile criticism, such as that by the anonymous memorandist, increasingly forced them to defend and justify it.

Spengler had good reason to fear the spread or even the public discussion of his friend's unorthodox opinions. While it is not clear whether those opinions had been advanced with the knowledge and support of others,[15] it is clear that there were in Nürnberg other prominent citizens equally unhappy with the progress of confessionalization who might well have sided with the anonymous memorandist if given the chance.[16] Their concerted opposition might seriously have impeded the work already under way on the preparation of a church ordinance. Moreover, in the spring of 1530 the city council of Nürnberg, like all other Protestant governments in the Empire, was preparing itself to render account to Emperor Charles V at the coming diet in Augsburg for all that it

---

[14] The proximate agent of transmission was Erasmus. See James M. Estes, "*Officium principis christiani*: Erasmus and the Origins of the Protestant State Church," *Archiv für Reformationsgeschichte* 83 (1992):49–72.

[15] In his letter to Veit Dietrich (see note 17), Spengler writes in the plural about "some of our people" who have fallen into error. On the other hand, in his much more detailed and intimate letter to Brenz (Document No. 1), Spengler writes in the singular of one person who has fallen into error, which tends to support the conclusion that the anonymous memorandist was a solitary figure.

[16] One of them was Hepstein (cf. note 7); and another was the distinguished jurist Christoph Scheurl. Both would subsequently oppose the issuance of the church ordinance of 1533.

had done with respect to the establishment of the Reformation in its territory. How could the council possibly justify its ban on Catholic doctrine and worship if its *cura religionis* were under attack by its own citizens or if it were even contemplating the toleration of Anabaptists and Jews? Spengler decided to forestall any such embarrassing developments by soliciting from experts learned memoranda that would refute the anonymous memorandist's views and provide an adequate theological justification for the magisterial Reformation and its official intolerance.

Accordingly, on 17 March 1530 Spengler wrote to Veit Dietrich, a former Nürnberger who was now Luther's confidant and personal secretary in Wittenberg, asking him to elicit Luther's opinion.[17] Luther, who was not sent the anonymous memorandum and who was apparently ill-informed about the summary of the anonymous author's views in Spengler's letter to Dietrich,[18] responded with an opinion that did not address the issues that were at stake in the Nürnberg controversy.[19] Meanwhile, at about the same time that he wrote to Dietrich in Wittenberg, Spengler also wrote to Brenz in Schwäbisch Hall, asking him to submit his written opinion of the anonymous author's memorandum, and sometime before 26 March Brenz agreed to do so.[20]

Brenz (1499–1570) was used to being asked to participate in theological discussions and debates in Nürnberg. In 1522, after several years as member of a humanist circle at the University of Heidelberg that produced a number of Protestant reformers (including Martin Bucer), he had become the city preacher in Schwäbisch Hall, a small imperial city that tended to follow the lead of Nürnberg in the affairs of the Empire. While leading the Reformation in Schwäbisch Hall, Brenz had also established himself both as a trusted adviser to Margrave George of the principality of Brandenburg-Ansbach and as a man whose views were

---

[17] WA 31/1:183–84.

[18] See Schmid, 305 note 83.

[19] Luther's response was incorporated into his commentary on the Eighty-Second Psalm, WA 31/1:207–13, AE 13:61–67.

[20] Spengler's original letter is lost, but in his letter of 26 March (Document No. 1) he acknowledges receipt of the "note," also lost, in which Brenz had agreed to submit his opinion. See p. 37.

esteemed by his fellow reformers in Nürnberg. By the time that Spengler solicited his intervention in the dispute with the anonymous memorandist, Brenz had, at Spengler's request, already written two memoranda on the treatment of Anabaptists, one in July 1528 and the other in March 1530.[21] In both cases he rejected toleration but also strongly objected to the use of the death penalty, a view that was shared by his Nürnberg colleagues. In the period 1530–33, Brenz participated, on the Ansbach side, in the preparation of the church ordinance that Margrave George and the Nürnberg city council issued jointly in 1533.

On 26 March 1530, Spengler dispatched to Brenz the letter that is Document No. 1 in this volume. He included with the letter a copy of the anonymous memorandum, to which was appended a letter to Spengler,[22] presumably by the same author.[23] Either with this letter or sometime in the weeks that followed, Spengler also sent to Brenz copies of two counter-memoranda (Documents Nos. 4 and 5) that he had procured from preachers in Nürnberg.[24] Before any of these documents were returned to Spengler, copies were made and retained in Schwäbisch Hall along with a copy of the memorandum that Brenz had written for Spengler (Document No. 3). While none of these documents, except for the anonymous memorandum, survives in the Nürnberg archives,[25] the Schwäbisch Hall copies have survived intact and constitute our principal documentary evidence regarding the Nürnberg controversy.[26]

---

[21] The texts are found in Brenz, *Frühschriften* 2: 480–98, 501–5. Summary and discussion in Estes, *Christian Magistrate* (Toronto, 1982), 44, 124–30.

[22] Included here as an addendum to Document No. 1.

[23] In his counter-memorandum (Document No. 3), Brenz treats both the memorandum and the appended letter as products of the same pen; see p. 62, paragraph 2.

[24] See the last sentence of Document No. 1, p. 40, with footnote 11.

[25] On the surviving Nürnberg manuscript (possibly the autograph) of the anonymous memorandum, see Osiander, *Gesamtausgabe* 3:631, note 2.

[26] Stadtarchiv Schwäbisch Hall, 4/55 (= Brentiana III); further details in notes 38, 39, 44, 46, 47. Another set of copies, apparently made in Schwäbisch Hall from the same originals as were the copies in the Hall archives and sent to the court at Brandenburg-Ansbach, with which Brenz had close connections, survives (poorly preserved and with pages missing) in the Staatsarchiv Bamberg. See Osiander, *Gesamtausgabe* 3:631, 635, 641. Cf. Schmid, 272–73 note 5.

Unfortunately, Spengler concealed from Brenz the identity of the authors of the documents sent to him, and the Hall copyist did not note which of the memoranda that he had copied was the one by Brenz. The still unsolved riddle of the authorship of the anonymous memorandum (Document No. 2) has been discussed above. Brenz's authorship of Document No. 3 has been established by the testimony of the eighteenth-century biographer of Spengler who possessed the autograph as well as Brenz's accompanying letter to Spengler.[27] It is from the same source that we learn that the memorandum was dated 8 May 1530.[28] As for the two counter-memoranda written by Nürnberg preachers (Documents 4 and 5), no satisfactory solution to the question of their authorship has yet been found. We know for sure that Andreas Osiander, preacher at St. Laurence's and the leading theologian in the city, wrote against the views expressed in the anonymous memorandum,[29] and there seems to be no reason to doubt that one of the two counter-memoranda sent to Brenz was Osiander's. The suggestion that Spengler himself may have written Document No. 5[30] has been convincingly refuted.[31] This has in effect narrowed the field of possible counter-memorandists down to Osiander and Wenzeslaus Linck, preacher at the Church of the Holy Spirit.

---

[27] U.G. Haußdorff, *Lebensbeschreibung eines christlichen Politici, nämlich Lazari Spengler* (Nürnberg: Johann Adam Schmidt, 1741), 322; cited in Brenz, *Frühschriften* 2: 509.

[28] Brenz, *Frühschriften* 2: 509–10.

[29] At the end of his letter to Spengler, the anonymous memorandist mentions "Osiander's memorandum." See p. 54.

[30] Brecht, "Gutachten," 66 and 74 note 24; Seebaß, 60.

[31] Osiander, *Gesamtausgabe* 3:636; Schmid, 292, esp. note 49. The argument is essentially (1) that Spengler would not have sent to Brenz a copy of a memorandum expressing views that he had already taken the trouble to outline in his letter of 26 March, especially if the memorandum had been included with the letter; and (2) that in Spengler's own catalogue of his papers he recorded no such memorandum by himself but did list "several memoranda by Nürnberg preachers," presumably those sent to Brenz. The "memorandum" by Spengler referred to in the second sentence of the anonymous memorandist's letter to Spengler (p. 52) must have been a summary of Spengler's position intended for the anonymous author alone.

Of these two, Osiander (1496–1552) was the better known and the more dominant figure. Educated at the University of Ingolstadt, Osiander took Reuchlin and Erasmus as his models and mastered all three ancient languages. Ordained in 1520, he began that year to teach Hebrew in the Augustinian monastery in Nürnberg and there came for the first time into contact with supporters of the Reformation. In 1522 he was appointed preacher at St. Laurence's and soon emerged as the undisputed leader of the reforming clergy and the most influential adviser of the city council on questions of theology and church order. He was the principal author of the church ordinance of 1533. Linck (1483–1547) was, like Luther, a Saxon and an Augustinian. He and Luther became close friends during their years together in Wittenberg (1508–16) in the Augustinian community and in the faculty of theology, and the two remained on intimate terms for the rest of Luther's life. Made preacher of the Augustinian cloister at Nürnberg in 1517, Linck left in 1520 to become vicar-general of the Augustinians and then in 1523 pastor in Altenburg, Saxony. In 1525 the Nürnberg city council appointed him to the preachership at the Church of the Holy Spirit, a post that he held until his death.

Returning to the question of who wrote what, the best guess for a time was that Documents Nos. 4 and 5 were by Linck and Osiander respectively.[32] But Hans-Ulrich Hofmann, who edited these texts for publication in the new critical edition of Osiander's works, has demonstrated just how uncertain this attribution is.[33] Hofmann's analysis indicates that, on the whole, the style and content of Document No. 4 support an attribution to Osiander while those of Document No. 5 support an attribution to Linck. But such attribution raises two problems that are not easily disposed of. The first problem is that if Osiander wrote Document No. 4, one has to explain how it was that he could cite a letter of Martin Luther to Wenzeslaus Linck as the answer to a question from himself.[34] The self-willed Osiander was far less likely than the

---

[32] Schmid, 292–94. For earlier guesses, see the references cited in note 30.

[33] See Osiander, *Gesamtausgabe* 3:635–38. What follows is a brief summary of Hofmann's analysis.

[34] Luther to Linck, 14 July 1528: "For when I asked the advice of Dr. Martin on this question, he replied in writing as follows...." See p. 90.

rather dependent Linck to solicit Luther's advice. The letter to Luther asking his opinion is lost, but Luther's reply to Linck[35] contains not so much as a word of greeting for Osiander. On the other hand, the author of the memorandum does not actually say that Luther wrote personally to him but only that Luther "replied in writing" to his question. This leaves open the possibility that Osiander asked Linck, who had closer personal contacts in Wittenberg than he did, to put the question to Luther without mentioning his name, though that would have been a most unusual procedure. The second problem is that on the manuscript of the anonymous memorandum in the Nürnberg archives there is a marginal gloss in Linck's handwriting that reads: "Luth[er]; Von weltlicher öbirkeit, C vide," i.e., "See Luther, *On Secular Authority*, [folio] C."[36] This was Linck's notation of a passage in Luther that could be used to counter the argument of the anonymous memorandist that the Old Testament is no longer binding. But the passage noted is cited only in the otherwise largely "Osiandrian" Document No. 4,[37] not in the more "Linckish" Document No. 5. It follows, then, that either of the two counter-memoranda can plausibly be attributed to either Osiander or Linck. For this reason, no firm attribution of either document to either man has been made in this volume.

Fortunately, all the documents presented here retain their interest and importance regardless of who may have written them. First of all, they deal with questions that faced virtually all the reformers and nearly all Protestant governments, not just those in Nürnberg: where exactly is the boundary between spiritual and secular authority? at what point does well-meaning governmental assistance in the process of reform become unwarranted interference in matters of faith and conscience? is the magisterial Reformation a theologically respectable enterprise or one that violates the norms laid down in scripture and the theology of Luther? Moreover, the answers provided by the three counter-memorandists, even though

---

[35] See p. 90 note 99.

[36] This corresponds to WA 11:255.31–256.7. Cf. AE 45:96–97. The same marginalium appears in the Schwäbisch Hall manuscript, but in Brenz, *Frühschriften* 2: 518, the Roman numeral "C" has been misread as "etc." and the Luther citation provided is not the appropriate one.

[37] See p. 79.

set down in documents that were neither published nor widely read, throw light on the general drift of thought among the Lutheran reformers that was to culminate in the mid-1530s in the "definitive" theological justification, by Philip Melanchthon, of the magisterial Reformation and its intolerance.

The documents before us are also interesting because they are the record of a controversy over religious freedom and the *cura religionis* of the magistrate that took place, not between representatives of the Protestant establishment on the one hand and spokesmen for radically dissident groups on the other, but within the Protestant establishment itself. The memorandum by the anonymous Nürnberger demonstrates that it was possible, at least in these early years, to articulate a potent case for freedom of religion on the basis of some of the fundamental principles of Luther's theology (albeit a one-sided reading of that theology in its earliest form). At the same time, however, the three counter-memoranda by Brenz and his two Nürnberg colleagues demonstrate that, granted the experiences and the presuppositions of sixteenth-century society, the weight of the evidence and the burden of justice were overwhelmingly on the side of intolerance.

The Content of the Documents

Because all the participants in this controversy, including the anonymous memorandist, operated within a world of thought and historical experience far removed from that of the English-speaking world in the late twentieth century, and because there are significant differences in the responses of the three counter-memorandists, the reader may find the following guide to the content of the documents helpful.

1. Spengler's letter to Brenz, 26 March 1530[38]

Evidently eager that Brenz should form as negative an opinion as possible of the views of the anonymous memorandist, Spengler

---

[38] *Ein schreiben Latzari Spenglers an seiner gueten freundt ainen mit beger, ihne zu berichten, ob ein obrigkhait gezwungen sey, die ketzer und verfüerer ihn ihren gebietten zu dulden oder nit.* Stadtarchiv Schwäbisch Hall 4/55:17 recto–19 verso. Printed in Brenz, *Frühschriften* 2: 512–16. Two earlier printed

not only forwards him a copy of the memorandum but also paints a lurid picture of the dangerous consequences of the toleration that the memorandist is advocating. The devil is at work here trying not only to undermine the efforts of government to establish unity and order in the true faith but even to undermine government itself. Toleration would give a free hand to every kind of idolater, deceiver, and heretic to work his mischief and lead pious Christian subjects astray. Worst of all, it would open the door to "the public abomination of the mass." Spengler cites the career of the revolutionary preacher, Thomas Müntzer, who is made to bear the blame for Anabaptism and the Peasants' Revolt, as evidence of the danger of tolerating the devil. Thus, while government is admittedly forbidden to put heretics to death, it must not on that account sit on its hands and impose no penalties at all. Spengler leaves it to Brenz to provide the theological justification for action to defeat the devil's tricks.

2. The Anonymous Memorandum (with the appended letter to Spengler), before 17 March 1530: *Whether Secular Government Has the Right to Wield the Sword in Matters of Faith*[39]

The author is appalled by the senseless torture, banishment, and execution of harmless persons throughout Germany and fears that unless governments cease their attempts to exterminate heresy by the sword, religious war will one day be the result. He takes aim at the two most widely-used arguments that contemporary governments and their theologians used to justify magisterial control of the public exercise of religion as well as the persecution of religious dissidents. The first was that the Christian magistrate, like the priest-kings of the Old Testament, is responsible to God for the religious as well as the secular welfare of his subjects and thus must assure that they are not only provided with true doctrine and worship but also protected from contamination by false doctrine and worship. The second argument rested on the assumption that a state divided in religion is ungovernable, not only because factional

---

versions are listed in ibid., 507.

[39] *Ob ein weltlich oberkait recht habe, in des glaubens sachen mit dem schwert zu handeln.* Stadtarchiv Schwäbisch Hall 4/55:20 recto–29 verso. First published in Brecht, "Gutachten," 67–75, and then in Brenz, *Frühschriften* 2: 517–28.

strife inevitably leads to civil strife but also because false doctrine and worship are a major source of civil disorder, as in the case of the Peasants' Revolt, which was commonly blamed on "false preachers." Hence, a government that wants to fulfil its duty to preserve civil peace and order must secure the confessional unity of its territory by promoting true preaching and worship while suppressing false teaching and ceremonies.[40]

The author tries to refute the first argument by declaring the Old Testament no longer binding on Christians and by insisting that the New-Testament teaching regarding the proper division between the spiritual and the secular realms must be strictly observed. He insists, citing scripture and using the language of Luther's doctrine of the two kingdoms,[41] that secular government may not interfere in the spiritual kingdom of faith and conscience, which is ruled solely by Christ through his word. But he parts company with Luther when he enlarges the concept of "spiritual kingdom" to include not just the inner realm of faith and con-science but also all external activities, especially preaching and worship, undertaken by the adherents of any faith, whether true or false. So when he speaks of "matters of faith," he is referring not merely to matters of inward, personal conviction but also to the whole public realm of religious and ecclesiastical affairs. Consequently, his demand that secular governments refrain from interference in Christ's kingdom is in fact a demand that they observe complete confessional neutrality and abstain from interfer-ence in the activities of any religious group. He does concede that a magistrate who is a Christian may act "as an individual person" to "further Christ's kingdom," and develops that point at some length in the appended letter to Spengler. But he condemns as wanton violation of Christ's kingdom any attempt by the magistrate to use his public office to compel acceptance of an official faith or conformity to the ceremonies and usages of an established church.

---

[40] For a summary of these arguments as formulated by Johannes Brenz, see Estes, *Christian Magistrate*, chapter 3.

[41] See Luther, *On Secular Authority* (1523) in AE 45:104ff. For an illuminating analysis of Luther's *Zwei-Reiche-Lehre*, see W.D.J. Cargill Thompson, *The Political Thought of Martin Luther* (Totawa, New Jersey: Barnes & Noble, 1984), chapter 3.

The author's critique of the second argument is less strictly theological and more empirical than that of the first. It is aimed primarily at allaying the fear of religious dissent by showing that there is in fact no cause-effect relationship between false doctrine and disorder or rebellion. Tumult, he says, is not caused by false faith or teaching but by evil men, who are to be found in all religious groups. Governments should punish the tumult but leave the peaceful adherents of a true or false faith undisturbed. Since insurgents take up the sword contrary to the will of God, God will surely give the sword of government victory over them. Thus fear of rebellion is groundless and no fit reason for doing violence in Christ's kingdom by persecuting the peaceful members of a false faith, especially since experience shows that such persecution only strengthens Anabaptists and other sectarians in their false faith. Indeed, Christ himself, his apostles, and the prophets before them were all the cause of tumult and were denounced as rebels. Should one on that account ban the teaching of the true faith? Besides, the example of the Kingdom of Bohemia, with its variety of Christian confessions and its Jewish community, shows that peace and order can be maintained in a country divided in religion. Government, therefore, should confine itself to the task of preserving external peace and order and leave false faith and worship to be dealt with in the spiritual kingdom by means of the word of God.

The task that the anonymous memorandist imposed on his adversaries was thus twofold. First, they had to demonstrate that the *cura religionis* of the magistrate was consistent with the proper distinction between spiritual and secular authority, and second, they had somehow to deal with the damage done to the presumed connection between false religion and public tumult. On the first issue, at least, they had a decided advantage over the anonymous author because their understanding of the relationship between secular and spiritual government was in fact far closer to Luther's than was his.

Although Luther was almost alone among Lutheran reformers in his unwillingness to assign routine authority over the church to secular authority per se,[42] he had nevertheless taken the lead in

---

[42] This is a big subject that cannot be gone into in any detail here. Suffice it to say (1) that Luther was virtually unique in not having come to the Reformation via Erasmian humanism and that he was thus not heir to the Erasmian notion

calling on secular authorities (most recently the elector of Saxony) to intervene in ecclesiastical affairs in the interest of orderly and effective reformation. In so doing, he had used arguments that his colleagues—Brenz, Osiander, Linck, and many others—could take over and use, along with arguments from other sources, for the purpose of defending the *cura religionis* of the magistrate. Luther, for example, chose to regard governmental measures to effect ecclesiastical reformation not as the exercise of routine secular authority in the church but rather as a service of love performed by leading members of the church who, by virtue of their participation in the priesthood of all believers, can, in an emergency, act for the entire community to curb abuses and inaugurate reform. Luther's colleagues, by contrast, simplified matters by appealing to the secular authorities *both* as secular rulers *and* as members of the church and by dropping the limitation to emergencies of secular intervention in the church's internal affairs. Again, while Luther did indeed insist that the secular and spiritual realms are distinct and that secular and spiritual authority must not be confused, he also maintained that both are of divine origin and that the proper functioning of each is essential to the welfare of the other. Freed of the limitations imposed in the context of Luther's own thought, this blended readily with his colleagues' predisposition to assign a specifically religious purpose to secular authority as such.

Perhaps even more important in the context of the debate in Nürnberg in 1530 is that if one accepted Luther's view that external ceremonies as such are neither sacred nor binding on conscience but are simply convenient external means for preaching the word and administering the sacraments, and if one agreed with him that secular authority extends to all external matters on earth, then one could conclude that all external aspects of church life were in the

---

of the Christian magistrate with authority in the sphere of religion (see above, note 14); (2) that Luther viewed secular authority as neither intrinsically nor necessarily Christian and had little faith in the good intentions of princes as a class; and (3) that Luther assigned routine authority in the church to the whole community of believers, not just to their political leaders. For a good general introduction to Luther's views on the relationship of church and state, see Cargill Thompson (as in the preceding note), chapters 8 and 9.

secular realm and thus subject to the authority of the Christian magistrate. Similarly, if Luther was right in arguing that a secular government that suppresses any religious activities that threaten temporal peace and order (e.g., the "public blasphemy" of the Roman mass, which arouses the wrath of God, or factious preaching, which leads to "mobs and rebellion") is not guilty of interfering in the spiritual realm because no one is thereby required to believe anything, then it would seem to follow that a magistrate who establishes and maintains true preaching and worship while leaving individuals free to believe as they wish in private is not interfering in spiritual matters either but simply doing his duty to promote peace and good order in his territory. Though Luther himself had not spelled out all these implications of his own thought, his colleagues, including the authors of the counter-memoranda under discussion here, had good reason to do so.[43]

3. Brenz's Counter-Memorandum, 8 May 1530: *An Answer to the Memorandum That Deals With This Question: Whether Secular Government Has the Right to Wield the Sword in Matters of Faith*[44]

Brenz readily concedes that the New Testament distinguishes between the spiritual and secular realms, each with its own distinct purpose and ruling authority, and that faith, whether true or false, is beyond the scope of secular authority. But he chides the author of the anonymous memorandum for failing to distinguish between true or false faith on the one hand and the works and deeds of true or false faith on the other. Faith in the heart and personal, private confession of that faith are not subject to the authority of secular government, but the formation of a new sect and the establishment of a new teaching office are the concern of the secular magistrate, to whom God has assigned the task of maintaining peace and order among Christians (1 Tim. 2:1–2). If the

---

[43] For an analysis of Luther's views considered from the point of view of their influence on Brenz and other advocates of the *cura religionis* of the magistrate, see Estes, *Christian Magistrate*, 19–28.

[44] *Antwort auff die vertzeichnus, so auff diße frag (Ob ein weltliche oberkait recht habe, in des glaubens sachen mit dem schwert zu handeln) gestellt ist.* Stadtarchiv Schwäbisch Hall 4/55:31 recto–42 verso. Printed in Brenz, *Frühschriften* 2: 528–41.

new doctrine and worship are useful and peaceful, the magistrate should defend and promote them, but if they are demonstrably scandalous and factious, then the magistrate must abolish them. The reason for this is that false teaching and worship are sources of civic disorder, as the Peasants' Revolt demonstrated. A government that abolishes false teaching and worship and punishes the obstinate teachers of false doctrine is only acting in restraint of external offences; private faith is unmolested and consciences are left free. Brenz is sufficiently consistent and fair-minded to admit that the same is true in the case of similar action by a heretical government against the adherents of the true faith. The control of the secular magistrate over externals is complete, even if that control is used unjustly to persecute the true faith. It is true that the apostles taught and preached contrary to the order established by their government, but they had a special commission from God to do so and could demonstrate it by performing miracles. Those who today wish to teach contrary to the order established by their government must be able to offer the same proof of their special calling. Legally called and appointed pastors, on the other hand, have no need to prove their calling in this way.

However, while Brenz thus has a fairly easy time squaring magisterial control of the externals of religion with the doctrine of the two kingdoms, he has a difficult time with the anonymous memorandist's denial of the presumed connection between false religion and public disorder. This is because he is trapped by his own definition of the office of magistrate as simply that of guardian of peace and order and thus cannot, at this stage in his career, justify magisterial regulation of religious life on any grounds other than the preservation of external peace. The result is that he has no really satisfactory answer to the anonymous memorandist's argument, bolstered by the concrete example of Bohemia, that governments can maintain peace and order while tolerating false doctrine and worship. Brenz admits that there are cases where a people divided in religion accepts a ruler on the condition that he recognize the right of every group to remain unmolested in the exercise of its own religion. He even concedes that a government may well have good reason to permit the establishment of a new sect, as was perhaps the case with the admission of the Jews into Frankfurt and Worms. But Brenz denies that rulers in whose territory religious unity has been established are obligated to permit the establishment of a new sect. If they were, some God-fearing bishop would certainly have denounced those early Christian emperors who issued decrees against various heresies; but the historians record no incidence of such a denunciation.

The trouble with this line of argument is that it amounts to an admission that there is no necessary connection between false preaching or worship and civic disorder. But if no such connection exists, then neither is there any connection between true preaching or worship and civic peace. And this means that Brenz's standard argument for the magistrate's control of ecclesiastical affairs has been fatally damaged. Why bother shouldering the burden of enforcing doctrinal and liturgical uniformity if peace and order can be kept without all that trouble and expense? The argument that the magistrate is not compelled to tolerate a new sect is no answer to that question. The best that Brenz is able to do here is to adduce the argument that secular government must prevent not only tumult but also indecency and public scandal, such as bigamy and cursing, and to claim that, even if the preaching or worship of a false sect produces no tumult, it does cause disorder, confusion, and discord. "Why [then] should the government not be entitled to intervene in the matter?" But "why not?" makes a rather weak case. What is needed is a good, strong, positive argument for government intervention and intolerance that does not hinge upon the maintenance of public order or decency. Brenz's Nürnberg colleagues were able to supply such an argument and in so doing contributed significantly to a process of rethinking on Brenz's part that subsequently enabled him to defend the *cura religionis* of the magistrate with more skill than he had manifested in his reply to the anonymous memorandist.[45]

---

[45] See Estes, *Christian Magistrate*, 43–54.

4. The First Nürnberg Counter-Memorandum, authorship uncertain (Andreas Osiander or Wenzeslaus Linck), before 26 March 1530: *Whether a Secular Government May Regulate Spiritual Matters, Restrain False Teaching, and Put Down Ungodly Abuses* (preceded by an introduction bearing the title: *An Admonition to Avoid Unnecessary and Vain Questions and Disputes....*)[46]

The lengthy and learned introductory *Admonition*, which is very much in the tradition of humanist criticism of scholastic theologians, is a warning against difficult and unnecessary questions and disputations that lead from the path of truth and produce confusion and error. The author sees the danger of such confusion and error lurking in disputes concerning the authority of secular government in spiritual matters and thus, in the first paragraph of the memorandum itself, he proclaims the necessity of proceeding solely on the basis of scripture accurately interpreted. He then sets out to demonstrate, point by point, that the anonymous memorandist has strayed from this path.

According to the author, the anonymous memorandist's basic mistake is to have attempted to isolate the spiritual and temporal realms from one another when in fact the two are bound together like body and soul in mutual dependence and service by Christ's commandment, equally applicable in both realms, to love God above all things and one's neighbour as one's self. From this perspective, the author attempts to correct the anonymous memorandist's interpretation of all those biblical passages that he had cited in support of his arguments. At the same time, while introducing some new biblical passages into the discussion (e.g., 1 Cor. 5:13, Matt. 18:6, and Deut. 13:1–5) and strenuously defending the relevance of the Old Testament, the author argues that although the word of God is the most effective weapon against false teaching, other methods have their place as well. Thus, just as Christ dealt with secular matters (marriage, taxes, the punish-

---

[46] *Ob ein weltliche oberkait in gaistlichen sachen moge ordnen, falsche ler wern und gotloss miszbreuch abstellen*, with the introductory section entitled: *Ein warnung, sich vor unnöttigem und vergeblichem fragen und disputiren zu hüeten, sintemal soliche anderst nichts dann ein verwirrung der sinn und falsche verfüerung mit sich bringen*. Stadtarchiv Schwäbisch Hall 4/55:43 recto–55 verso. Published in Osiander, *Gesamtausgabe* 3:642–55.

ment of crimes) in a spiritual way, so secular government may, where love and necessity require, intervene in spiritual matters, using its own secular means, but acting to serve faith and promote the glory of God. It would be interference in God's realm if the government sought to rule consciences, but public preaching is in the external realm and thus subject to governmental regulation.

The author deals with the anonymous memorandist's denial of the causal connection between false doctrine and tumult by declaring the question irrelevant. It makes no difference, he insists, whether false doctrine causes disorder and tumult or not: the protection of the truth and the punishment of error for the sake of the glory of God constitute the real reason for governmental intervention in religious matters (Rom. 13:4, 6), not the preservation of external peace and order. Indeed, even if false doctrine were (contrary to all reasonable expectation) to bring great temporal benefits or if, by contrast, the persecution of heretics were to result (as predicted by the anonymous memorandist) in an alarming increase in their numbers, a Christian government would still be obligated to uphold truth and the glory of God. The only limitation on governmental action against false teaching (apart from avoiding the death penalty) is that the government must act on the basis of certain knowledge of the truth and not intervene hastily and without reflection in spiritual matters.

Christian governments have the right, indeed the duty, to establish and enforce true preaching and worship, and no one has the right to resist them or to conspire against them on that account unless, like the apostles, they have a special commission from God to do so. A government cannot observe neutrality in religious matters without abandoning its obligation to rule according to the will and law of God (Deut. 17:18–19) and, indeed, without rendering itself superfluous. If a government must permit the unhindered exercise of the vices of false and deceitful preaching and worship, on what grounds can it take action against other offences, which only harm the body and not the soul or the glory of God? In other words, the demand for the freedom of religion for all Christian sects as well as Jews is, in fact, a demand for the restoration of the old and much resented exemption of the clergy from secular authority in a new and particularly chaotic form.

5. The Second Nürnberg Counter-Memorandum, authorship uncertain (Wenzeslaus Linck or Andreas Osiander), before 26 March 1530: *Whether Secular Christian Government Has the Power to Ban False Preachers or Erring Sects and to Establish Order in Ecclesiastical Affairs* [47]

This is by far the longest of the documents in the controversy and in many ways the most interesting and accomplished as well. The author's views are essentially the same as those found in the preceding memorandum, but they are supported by an analysis that is even more thorough and by the adduction of additional biblical evidence (especially from Psalm 2 and the Wisdom of Solomon) to bolster the claim that secular government was established to promote and defend the spiritual realm. Moreover, of the three counter-memoranda, this one is the least constrained by the format of point-by-point refutation of the memorandum of the anonymous Nürnberger and comes closest to being an independent, internally coherent examination of the whole question of the office of the secular magistrate in matters of religion. On the other hand, the author's love of long-winded and convoluted discourse, his propensity for repetition, and his tendency to get lost in the intricacies of his own prose frequently make his line of reasoning difficult to follow. Nevertheless, the basic structure of his argument is quite simple.

While readily conceding that the authority of secular government extends only to external human affairs, he insists, citing Rom. 13:3–4, that the secular realm was established not for its own sake but to serve the kingdom of God. Thus his concern is not to exalt secular government per se but only to explain to God-fearing Christian rulers how to make proper use of their authority. His thesis is that all things that pertain directly to the spiritual realm should be dealt with in a spiritual manner by the clergy, but that those same things, to the extent that they are external and separable from the spiritual realm, should be dealt with by the Christian magistrate "for the promotion and protection of the truth."

---

[47] *Ob die weltlich, cristenlich oberkait gewalt hab, falsch lerer oder irrig secten zu wern und in gaistlichen sachen der kirchenbreuch zu ordnen etc.* Stadtarchiv Schwäbisch Hall 4/55:56 recto–74 verso. Printed in Osiander, *Gesamtausgabe* 3:656–73.

Before going on to prove this thesis, the author devotes several paragraphs to making four points in elucidation of its content. First, all external ceremonies and practices that have been established by human action and contribute nothing to salvation are ipso facto worldly things that fall by definition under the authority of secular government even though papal laws may have unjustly reserved control of them to the clergy. This is not the case, however, with respect to public preaching and the administration of the sacraments, which are external deeds but which Christ himself has established in his kingdom as part of the spiritual government of souls. Second, the bible forbids the officials of either kingdom, spiritual or temporal, to usurp the office of those of the other kingdom. Third, it is nevertheless appropriate for a Christian ruler to use his secular office for the promotion and protection of the spiritual realm. Fourth, everything that is external and known to secular government falls under its authority, for even the holiest and most spiritual people are at the same time carnal and thus subject to secular authority, along with everything external that they have or do.

Then comes the demonstration of the thesis in two extended sections, the second much longer than the first. First, St. Paul and other New-Testament writers teach that the real worship of God is entirely internal and spiritual and beyond human power. The worldly sword can do nothing in spiritual matters, for it cannot even know them. At the same time, however, public teaching and preaching, though they pertain to the kingdom of God, are also external deeds and thus in the realm of secular government. This raises the difficult question of who should have authority over them. Second, scripture teaches that the secular and spiritual realms are not opposed to one another like Christ and Satan but rather are bound together and serve one another like law and gospel or body and soul. Jesus supported and promoted the secular realm and, similarly, secular government is God's minister for the promotion and protection of the spiritual realm (Rom. 13:4, 1 Tim. 2:1–4). God has condemned the tyrannical misuse of secular authority, but he has also specifically commanded all kings and other secular rulers to serve his kingdom and has threatened them with his wrath if they do not do so (Ps. 2:10–12, Wisd. 6:1–5). Old-Testament kings (the relevance of the Old Testament is once again strenuously defended) were praised because they silenced false teachers and destroyed false worship. But the New Testament allows secular rulers even greater leeway because it gives them unfettered authority to act in spiritual matters to the extent that the love of God and of their fellow Christians demands. The only proviso is that they act within the limits of their secular calling (i.e., without usurping the pastoral office or otherwise interfering in the realm of private faith) and that their actions truly benefit the kingdom of God rather than their own worldly ambition or greed.

In sum: preaching and teaching are external works; true preaching is a good work that builds the kingdom of God while false preaching is an evil work that injures the glory of God. Thus secular rulers should see to the training and appointment of true and qualified preachers and to the restraint or dismissal of the teachers of false doctrine (who are in any case completely carnal, without the spirit of God, and thus outside his kingdom). This is not interference in God's kingdom; it is merely the exercise of God-given secular authority in the secular realm in accordance with the true purpose of that authority: the service of Christ and his kingdom.

The historical significance of the documents in this volume does not lie in any commotion or discussion that they provoked at the time. The anonymous Nürnberger did not offer his views to the public at large and neither did any of the counter-memorandists. Spengler succeeded in forestalling a potentially dangerous attack on the emerging church order in Nürnberg, and that was that. The memoranda quickly disappeared into the archives and had no further effect on the course of the Reformation. The significance of the documents is, rather, that they provide an unusually good and relatively brief introduction to the problems involved in justifying the *cura religionis* of the magistrate and to the search for credible solutions to those problems.

The basic problem facing the Lutheran reformers in their defence of the magisterial Reformation and the intolerance that it espoused was to demonstrate that governmental intervention in matters of faith was consistent with the fundamental distinction between the secular and spiritual realms. Part of the demonstration consisted of showing that the church on earth is itself located simultaneously in *both* realms and that it is therefore not a purely spiritual institution but one whose external trappings (often conventionally referred to as "spiritual matters" or "matters of faith") are, to the extent that they are external, worldly matters subject to the control of secular government. But for this to make any sense at all from the point of view of the aims and purposes of the spiritual realm, it had also to be shown that the two realms have the same purpose, namely the glory of God and the salvation of souls, and that God requires Christian secular rulers to govern the secular realm in such a way as to promote and protect the spiritual realm or, to put it another way, to serve the church and their fellow Christians by establishing and defending true doctrine and worship and by abolishing false doctrine and worship. Thus to achieve their purpose, the reformers had to assign to secular government a much loftier goal than simply that of preserving external peace. It was too easy, as the anonymous memorandist had demonstrated, to demolish the presumed connection between true religion and peace, false religion and disorder. Moreover, in justifying this lofty goal, the reformers had to find in scripture actual divine commandments to kings, princes, and other secular rulers to establish and enforce true doctrine and worship and to punish heretics. Simply to demonstrate that the doctrine of the two kingdoms posed no obstacle to secular intervention in the externals of religion provided rather too negative and weak an argument. It was more effective, in other words, to be able to say: "this is what God demands of you, on pain of your soul's salvation" than to be able to say only: "you won't violate the spiritual kingdom if you do such and such." Finally, to make a convincing scriptural argument that God himself had imposed the establishment and defence of true religion upon secular rulers, it was of course necessary to uphold the continuing validity of the Old Testament, where the vast majority of the best supporting texts were to be found, though key passages in the New Testament were pressed into service as well.

Of the three men who wrote responses to the memorandum of the anonymous Nürnberger, it is the two Nürnberg preachers who come closest to meeting all these challenges adequately. The second Nürnberg counter-memorandum, in particular, comes reasonably close to stating what would become the standard view of the office of Christian magistrate in Lutheran Germany. Indeed, it is not too much to claim that the author, in his own long-winded and convoluted way, is saying essentially what Philip Melanchthon would, starting in 1535,[48] say with such ingenious brevity and clarity (and with much fuller scriptural and historical evidence): that the secular magistrate is the guardian, with respect to external discipline (i.e., in the secular realm) of both tables of the law (i.e., of the true worship of God, covered in the first table of the Decalogue, and of decency and order in human affairs, covered in the second table), and that the first table is by far the more important.[49] In so doing, the Nürnberg author already exploits some of the same biblical texts (especially Ps. 2:10–12, Wisd. 6:1–5, Rom. 13:3–4, 1 Tim. 2:1–4) and interprets them in the same way as would Melanchthon and, after Melanchthon, hordes of Protestant preachers and theologians, including Johannes Brenz.[50] By the 1540s, any competent preacher who had read the right textbooks could demonstrate conclusively that religious intolerance was the solemn duty of every Christian magistrate and that toleration was wicked, inhuman, and dangerous.

In conclusion, it is perhaps appropriate to insert a word of qualification about what has been said above concerning the connection between true doctrine and worship on the one hand and secular peace and order on the other. The assertion of an automatic and necessary connection between the two was, as we have seen, a fallible argument in the context of theological debate. Nevertheless, the theologians continued to see a connection between temporal peace and the true worship of God. Brenz, for example, in his later works on the office of magistrate, subordinated the task of maintaining peace and order to that of serving the church but at the same time cited biblical and historical

---

[48] In the edition of the *Loci communes* of that year and in all subsequent editions. The German edition of 1555 is available in an English version translated and edited by Clyde Manschreck: *Melanchthon on Christian Doctrine: Loci Communes of 1555* (New York: Oxford UP, 1965). See pp. 323–43 for the chapter "Of Worldly Authority."

[49] Melanchthon's most thorough examination of this subject was *De officio principum, quod mandatum Dei praecipiat eis tollere abusus Ecclesiasticos*, published in 1539 in response to Catholic apologists who denied that princes had the authority to proceed independently with the reform and reorganization of the churches in their territories; see *Melanchthons Werke in Auswahl*, ed. Robert Stupperich et al. (Gütersloh: C. Bertelsmann, 1951ff.), 1:387–410.

[50] See Estes, *Christian Magistrate*, 52–58.

evidence in support of the claim that those states that benefit the church endure while those that persecute it decline.[51] Even more significant was that contemporaries in general clung to the assumption of a direct and simple connection between true religion on the one hand and temporal well being on the other. In this view, a government that took action against false teaching or ungodly worship was not simply serving God's kingdom but was also protecting its subjects against the inescapable temporal punishments (war, famine, pestilence, etc.) that God would inflict on a land that tolerated such things. It took this idea a long time to die—it endured well into the Age of Reason and beyond—and while it lived, it powerfully reinforced the atmosphere of intolerance that the theologians had learned to justify on more sophisticated grounds.

Translator's Note

With the exception of the memorandum of the anonymous Nürnberger (Document No. 2), all the translations are published here for the first time. My translation of the anonymous memorandum was first printed in the *Mennonite Quarterly Review* 49 (1975):22–37, and is republished here, in revised form, with the kind permission of the editors of that journal. All the translations, including the revised version of that of the anonymous memorandum, are based on the texts in Brenz, *Frühschriften* 2 (for documents 1, 2, 3) and Osiander, *Gesamtausgabe* 3 (for documents 4, 5). I have, however, occasionally made small corrections based on the Schwäbisch Hall manuscripts. Moreover, I have not necessarily accepted the judgment of the German editors with respect either to the meaning of obscure passages or to the interpolation of modern punctuation (especially in the case of their use of quotation marks around biblical citations, many of which I have felt compelled to treat as close paraphrases rather than direct quotations).

In order to get sixteenth-century German into readable modern English, I have sometimes had to translate very freely. Only where the meaning of the original German was in doubt, however, have I attempted to justify my freedom in a footnote. Editorial emenda-

---

[51] Estes, *Christian Magistrate*, 56.

tions that were required to clarify the meaning of the text or to fill in obvious gaps have been placed in square brackets. Only where the emendations are not self-explanatory have I added a footnote commentary. In rendering biblical passages, whether as paraphrases or as quotations, I have freely adapted the texts of either the Authorized Standard (King James) Version or the Revised Standard Version (or a combination of both) in order to produce something close to the rhetoric of the English Bible while still doing justice to the meaning of the author's (sometimes idiosyncratic) German version. Where the author's interpretive point is supported only by one particular version of the passage in question, that version has been specified in a footnote.

Both in the introduction and in the notes I have borrowed freely from the introductory material and the notes in Brenz, *Frühschriften* 2 and Osiander, *Gesamtausgabe* 3. The labours of the German editors of those two editions made my task much easier than it otherwise would have been and undoubtedly made the result more accurate as well. Moreover, two of those colleagues have generously provided further assistance. Martin Brecht, co-editor of the Brenz edition, read the entire manuscript of the translated documents. His frank and detailed comments saved me from a few truly egregious errors, provided the solutions to a number of difficult problems of interpretation, and made possible many less momentous improvements as well. Gottfried Seebaß, one of the general editors of the Osiander edition, not only responded to my inquiries about certain aspects of the Nürnberg counter-memoranda but undertook to read and criticize the first draft of the introduction as well. His comments and suggestions made possible substantial improvements to both content and organization. Erika Rummel, editor of C.R.R.S. Texts in Translation Series, as well as the anonymous colleague who refereed the manuscript, also made a number of suggestions that led to improvements in both the introduction and the translations. I am grateful to all these colleagues for their help but naturally would not wish them to be held responsible for any errors or other deficiencies that remain as the result of my own folly.

It is a pleasant duty to acknowledge that this book has been published with the help of a grant from the Canadian Federation for the Humanities, using funds provided by the Social Sciences and Humanities Research Council of Canada.

Select Bibliography

In addition to the titles listed in Abbreviations (p. 7), the following can be recommended. For the history of the Reformation in Nürnberg, see Gottfried Seebaß, "The Reformation in Nürnberg," *The Social History of the Reformation,* ed. Lawrence P. Buck and Jonathan W. Zophy (Columbus, Ohio: Ohio State UP, 1972), 17–40; and Gerald Strauss, *Nuremberg in the Sixteenth Century* (New York/London: John Wiley & Sons, 1966), esp. chapter four. See also Harold J. Grimm, *Lazarus Spengler: A Lay Leader of the Reformation* (Columbus, Ohio: Ohio State UP, 1978). On the general problem of toleration and the *cura religionis* of the magistrate, see Joseph Lecler, S.J., *Toleration and the Reformation,* vol. 1 (New York: Association Press, 1960), trans. T.L. Westow, esp. books 2, 3, and 4; and W.D.J. Cargill Thompson, *The Political Thought of Martin Luther* (Totawa, New Jersey: Barnes & Noble, 1984), esp. chapters 8 and 9 (chapter 8 includes useful information on the views of Philip Melanchthon). See also Roland H. Bainton, *Studies on the Reformation* (Boston: Beacon Press, 1963), 20–45: "Luther's Attitudes on Religious Liberty."

Document Number One

A letter of Lazarus Spengler to one of his good
friends with the request that that friend inform him
whether or not a government is obliged to tolerate
heretics and deceivers in its territories

Highly esteemed, dear gentleman and brother, I have received your
note via Hans[1] and am extremely pleased that you will undertake
to send me your opinion concerning the problem about which I
have written to you. And I ask you as a brother to spare no effort
or industry in doing so. For truly, as you can imagine, much is at
stake here. For it seems to me that the devil wants to open a terrible
breach in our ranks, so that the word of God, true uniform religion,
Christian order, and the power and sword of secular government will
be completely reduced to rubble. And so that you might be able to
deal all the more thoroughly with this matter and to support all your
arguments, I am enclosing the memoranda[2] of the man who has fallen
into this opinion and who otherwise is truly an upright man and like
a brother to me. This very day I have had a long discussion of these
matters with him, in the attempt to move him from his current position
or, much more, from new errors, from which, as I fear and already
perceive, he will fall into even greater errors.

Several persons with knowledge of these matters have already
written against him.[3] But he adheres to his established opinion with
imposing firmness.

---

[1] Unidentified.

[2] Spengler is apparently counting the anonymous memorandum and the
letter appended to it (here combined as Document No. 2) as two memoranda.

[3] Presumably the counter-memoranda found here as Documents 4 and 5.

I asked him, among other things, if he could show me a single passage in all of scripture where government is required to tolerate public deceivers and seducers in matters of faith, false prophets, idolaters, blasphemers, and defilers of the gospel, and is forbidden to impose punishments (i.e., those short of public execution) on them. He replied that I had to concede that there are two kingdoms, spiritual and secular, and that the kind of errors that I had listed belong in God's kingdom, in which no government has the right to interfere. Now I admit that no government is entitled to compel anyone by force in matters of faith—indeed that it *cannot* do so—or to impose the death penalty for false belief. But if a government were absolutely required to tolerate in its territory those incontrovertibly recognized as public idolaters, deceivers, and heretics, whether they be pagans, Jews, or Christians, and to allow discordant preaching, idolatry, rebaptizing, and polluted sacraments and ceremonies, above all the public abomination of the mass,[4] in the churches, houses, cloisters, or assemblies under its jurisdiction, just imagine what improprieties would result and what would, in time, become of all authority. Governments would be compelled willy-nilly to tolerate the public enemies, defilers, and persecutors of God and his word, as well as the greatest enemies and opponents of government itself, and to permit them to work their mischief and to lead astray pious, Christian, obedient subjects. And when would one ever again be able to maintain a uniform Christian order and a unanimous godly religion in any territory if one had to tolerate all these scoundrels and deceivers and could not expel them? What would be the need or use of

---

[4] Because the Catholic mass was understood to be a mystical reenactment of Christ's sacrifice on the cross, and because its celebration was deemed to be a good work offered to God in order to earn merit, Protestants regarded it as a denial of the unique and universally effective nature of the original sacrifice on Calvary and of the biblical truth (as they saw it) that the salvation thereby achieved was available only through faith, not through the performance of meritorious works. On both counts, it was blasphemous and thus to be abominated. Moreover, because adoration was offered to the consecrated elements, the celebration of mass was denounced as idolatry. Wherever Protestantism challenged the old order, the abolition of mass was the primary goal of the reformers.

visitation ordinances[5] if it were in the power of every non-Christian or deceiver, without fear of governmental interference, to bring down that established order once more by means of offensive sermons, idolatries, and other such deeds in the government's own land and territories?

In my view, the fanaticism of Thomas Müntzer,[6] which alone initially awoke the Anabaptists, the sacrament polluters and, wantonly, the entire peasant rebellion, should be sufficient reason not to tolerate the devil, who is a liar and murderer,[7] until at length he puts his lying and murder into practice. Such toleration would be tempting God rather than trusting him, who has entrusted government with the sword not only for the protection of good people but even more because of evil people,[8] who are a much larger group. And in my opinion it is a bad argument that my brother has, among other arguments, used orally against me, to wit: because government is forbidden to put to death any heretic or anyone else for reasons of faith, it follows that government may impose no other penalty upon them or expel them but must tolerate them in its territory; otherwise there would be no restraint in such matters and the papists would be given grounds to treat us in the same way and observe no restraint. If this argument were valid, then it would necessarily follow that because under secular law secular government is forbidden to impose the death penalty for mere drunkenness, it therefore cannot impose any penalty at all. And what is it to me what adversaries or papists would do to us in similar circumstances? I am obligated, regardless of that, to

---

[5] In 1528 the city of Nürnberg and the neighbouring principality of Brandenburg-Ansbach had conducted a joint ecclesiastical visitation of their territories in the attempt to establish uniform standards of doctrine and practice; see Emil Sehling et al., eds., *Die evangelischen Kirchenordnungen des 16. Jahrhunderts* 11/1 (Tübingen: J.C.B. Mohr (Paul Siebeck), 1961):113–16.

[6] The radical reformer, Thomas Müntzer, who was beheaded in May 1525 for his role in the Peasants' Revolt, had resided in Nürnberg in 1524/25 and found some supporters there. Spengler's designation of Müntzer as the person solely responsible for the "fanaticism" of the Anabaptists and the rebellious peasants was as unjust as it was typical of Lutheran opinion at the time.

[7] See John 8:44.

[8] See Rom. 13:3–4.

do my duty and leave the godless to God. Spiritual government is always obligated to serve secular government and the secular realm is obligated to serve the spiritual realm. In sum, you as an expert judge will, I have no doubt, easily perceive that this is a concealed trick of the devil no matter how good its outward appearance may be.

I have hitherto most loyally advised my lords of the city council against soiling their hands with the blood of poor blind people like the Anabaptists and others, regardless of all the solemn mandates of the imperial government[9] or the league,[10] and would still offer the same advice. But I do not know how I could possibly justify advising them to tempt God openly by sitting on their hands and doing nothing.

[Here eight paragraphs dealing with matters unrelated to the question of the anonymous memorandist and his views have been omitted.]

Dated Saturday, 26 March 1530. In haste, as you see. Lazarus Spengler, Secretary to the City Council.

Please return the enclosed memoranda[11] along with your own memorandum.

---

[9] I.e., the Mandate Against the Anabaptists (23 April 1529), enacted by the Diet at Speyer.

[10] I.e., the Swabian League, an alliance of South-German princes and cities of which Nürnberg was a member.

[11] This vague reference in the plural to "beygelegte verzaichnus" can be read in two ways. On the one hand, it could mean simply that Spengler enclosed both of the anonymous memorandist's "memoranda," i.e., the memorandum proper plus the appended letter, which Brenz refers to as the author's "second memorandum" (see p. 62, and cf. above, note 2). On the other hand, it could also mean that Spengler enclosed the two Nürnberg counter-memoranda (i.e. Documents 4 and 5) as well as the anonymous memorandum with this letter; see introduction, p. 15. The problem with the latter reading is that in his own memorandum Brenz betrays not the slightest evidence of having read the memoranda of his two Nürnberg colleagues, which contain arguments that he might well have used or seconded. This makes one suspect that, in correspondence now lost, he requested and received copies of the Nürnberg memoranda after he had written and submitted his own.

Document Number Two

Whether Secular Government Has the Right to
Wield the Sword in Matters of Faith
[By an Anonymous Nürnberger,
before 17 March 1530]

There is simply no end to executions and banishments for reasons
of faith. Lutheran governments will not tolerate Anabaptists or
Sacramentarians.[1] Zwinglian governments also refuse to tolerate
Anabaptists. Then come the papists, who burn, hang, or banish
evangelicals, Lutherans, Zwinglians, Anabaptists and everyone
who is not of their faith.

The papists have, I believe, no other grounds for such behaviour
than their worthless [canon] law.[2] If they persist and refuse to heed
God's word or even reason and justice, then one must let them go
their way as long as God permits it.

But from those governments that are evangelical, Lutheran,
Zwinglian, and claim to hear God's word, to follow it, and in no
way to act contrary to it, even though papal law, as well as imperial
laws made under the papacy,[3] demand something else (as indeed
all laws, ordinances, and customs should rightly yield before God's
word): from those governments, I say, I would very much like to
hear where they get the right to control faith either by executing
those who do not wish to be of their faith or else by tearing them
from property and goods, wife and children, and banishing them
from the territory.

---

[1] I.e., Zwinglians.

[2] Cf. *Corpus juris canonici, Decretales Gregorii* IX 5.7.8–9.

[3] *Corpus juris civilis, Codex Iustinianus* 1.5.3ff.

So far as I know, the only justification that has been offered for this is the opinion of some people that since it is the duty of every government to protect its subjects in temporal matters pertaining to body and goods, so that no harm befall them, it behooves government to an even greater degree to do the same in spiritual matters, since these things have to do with faith and the highest good, in order that its subjects not be contaminated or led astray.

But if you ask them to cite scripture in support of this opinion, either no one is at home or else they refer us to the Old-Testament record of the Jewish kings who supported true worship, abolished idolatrous worship, and destroyed idols. If you reply that the Old Testament and Jewish law are no longer binding,[4] and that they should show where in the New Testament the secular government is commanded to be responsible for faith or to punish unbelievers with force or with the sword, then they are stuck.

Now it is certainly true that the Old Testament no longer binds anyone, and if we are bound in one matter on the ground that it is commanded in the Old Testament, how shall we avoid being bound in other such matters? If one thing were necessary, they would all be necessary, as Paul clearly concludes in Gal. 5[:3] and says against those who wanted to make circumcision obligatory that whoever has himself circumcised is obliged to fulfil the whole law. Therefore we must not be bound by anything in the Old Testament but rather give heed to the New Testament.

But the New Testament speaks of two kingdoms on earth, namely the spiritual and the secular. The spiritual kingdom is the kingdom of Christ in which Christ is king. Similarly, the secular realm also has its king, namely the emperor and other authorities. Just as each kingdom has its own distinct king, so each has its own distinct sceptre, goal, and end. The sceptre of the spiritual realm is the word of God; the goal and end to which this sceptre should attract and move us is that men turn to God and after this life be saved. The sceptre of the secular realm, on the other hand, is the

---

[4] The author is alluding to Luther, *Unterrichtung, wie sich die Christen in Mosen sollen schicken* (1525), WA 16:373.3f and 21f. But here Linck noted in the margin of the manuscript in the Nürnberg Archives a passage in Luther's *On Secular Authority* that could be used to refute the anonymous author's point; see the introduction, p. 18, with footnotes 36 and 37.

sword; the goal and end toward which it should drive and force men is that external peace be maintained.

That this is the proper division and distinction between the two kingdoms is powerfully demonstrated in the New Testament, where Christ and his agents, the apostles, observe the order of his kingdom most precisely, ruling in no other wise than with their sceptre, the word of God. With this word they teach, admonish, and censure men, and proclaim that he who accepts and believes it will be saved, while he who does not will be damned.[5] This is their method of government; they leave it at that and thereby their office is fulfilled. Nowhere does one find that if someone did not adhere to their doctrine and preaching but rather believed or taught some other faith, that they appealed to the secular government either to force such a person to accept their faith or else not to tolerate him. Nor does one find anywhere in the New Testament that any government that did this of its own accord was praised for it. On the contrary, Christ forbids it, as can be especially well observed in his explanation of his parable of the good seed and the tares, Matt. 13[:24–30, 37–43], where he says that the good seed are the children of the kingdom, sown by the Son of Man; the tares are the children of evil, sown by the devil; the harvest is the end of the world, the reapers the angels. He concludes that the tares should not be rooted up but rather allowed to remain, lest the wheat also be rooted up with them. For just as the tares are gathered and burned in the fire, so it will be at the end of the world: the Son of Man will send his angels, who will gather out of his kingdom all those that offend and cast into the furnace all those that work iniquity.

From this it is clear that Christ does not wish the sword of the secular government to be used to root anything out of his kingdom, but wishes rather to do combat there solely by his word until the end of the world. As the prophet Isaiah proclaims and says, Christ will do battle "with the breath of his mouth and with the rod of his lips,"[6] not with the sword of secular government. Here it is clearly stated that Christ himself will fight, not the secular govern-

---

[5] Mark 16:16.

[6] Isa. 11:4, where the prophet actually says "with the rod of his mouth and with the breath of his lips."

ment for him, with the rod of his mouth and with the breath of his lips, not with the sword of secular government. The prophet Daniel agrees with this and says that Antichrist (that is, all that sets itself against Christian faith and doctrine) shall be destroyed "without hand."[7] Whoever, then, seeks by secular power to defend true faith and doctrine or to drive out false faith and doctrine does nothing else than despise and mock the entire New Testament and the prophets as well. And, contrary to what Isaiah and Daniel say—that Christ will do battle in his kingdom by the breath of his mouth and that Antichrist will be destroyed without [human] hand—he also falsely maintains that the breath of Christ's mouth does not do it and that one must accomplish it with one's hand.

Furthermore, Christ and his apostles not only observe the order of his kingdom, they also leave the secular government completely unhindered in the possession of its kingdom. For when a man appealed to Christ to make his brother divide an inheritance with him, Christ refused in serious words saying: "Man, who made me a judge over you?"[8] And before Pilate he said: "My kingdom is not of this world."[9] He also taught his disciples, saying: "The secular kings exercise lordship and the mighty are called gracious lords. But ye shall not be so!" etc.[10] From this one sees how God wishes to have the two kingdoms distinguished from one another. And since Christ remains in his kingdom and lets the secular kingdom go its own way, even though he is far mightier than all emperors and kings, it is all the more proper that the secular government should take care of its own kingdom and not attempt to govern that which belongs to Christ.

Therefore, the sum and substance of the whole matter is this, that a government that wishes to discharge its office and not claim more than has been entrusted to it should and must leave it entirely to Christ the king to determine and judge, by means of the sceptre of his divine word, whether any teaching about faith, how man may come to God and be saved, be true or false. Just as one clearly sees that in his kingdom Christ does both things, namely, teaches

---

[7] Dan. 8:25 (ASV); the RSV is wordier but clearer: "by no human hand."
[8] Luke 12:14.
[9] John 18:36.
[10] Luke 22:25–26.

the true faith and condemns the false, pours the holy spirit into the heart and drives the devil out, doing both through his sceptre, the word, and calls on no secular authority to assist. Hence it is not proper for secular authority to do this. Rather it should use its sceptre or sword in the secular realm against external misdeeds, so that no one may be harmed in his body or goods. In such matters the secular sword is effective and God has established it for that reason. But the sword is of no use in forcing people to adhere to this or that faith. In the final analysis, whether you hang or drown them, the choice must still be left to those who do not want to go to heaven to go down to hell to the devil or his mother instead.

But someone may object that this is too crudely put, and that while it might perhaps be appropriate for a Turkish or heathen government to ignore the spiritual welfare of its subjects, a Christian government must not allow its subjects to be led astray by false doctrine. Answer: we have already heard that Christ, the king in the spiritual realm, not only gives true faith and the holy spirit but also drives out false faith and the devil. Now, just as it is neither right nor possible for the secular government, by means of its sceptre of the sword, to give anyone true faith or the holy spirit, so also it is neither right nor possible to drive out false faith, heresy, or the devil by means of the sword. Thus Turkish, heathen, Christian, and popish governments all have exactly the same authority. And both things, namely fighting for or against the true faith, the one as well as the other, constitute interference in Christ's kingdom and rebellion against it. If a government wishes to be Christian and further Christ's kingdom, it may do so as an individual person, but its office remains the same one way or the other. And if it is not proper for Turks and heathen to meddle in Christ's kingdom with the sword, it is even less so for a Christian government. But a Christian government can choose another course of action that is consistent with Christ's kingdom, namely by appointing good preachers who do battle by means of the word of God. Likewise, if it personally wishes to bring others from false faith to Christ, let it remain under the kingdom of Christ, use his sceptre, the word, and not have recourse to its sword in the secular kingdom.

But someone may say: you have said long and loud that the government should not interfere in the teaching of faith or unbelief, but much tumult arises where more than one faith is tolerated, and this a government must not allow. Answer: to be sure, a government must not tolerate tumult. But tumult, even if more dangerous things occur along with it, is no ground for transgressing upon Christ's kingdom and thus engaging in tumult oneself. For tumult and other crimes are caused not by true or false faith or doctrine but solely by evil men, who are to be found everywhere, among Christians and non-Christians, true and false believers. Tumult also arose because of Christ and his apostles, and before that because of the prophets, even though they taught the true faith, so that they were condemned as rebels. Would it therefore have been proper to destroy their faith and the teaching of it? And why speak of the old histories? Is it not the case in our own times that the Peasants' Revolt broke out because of the gospel before anyone had ever heard of any Anabaptist in our lands? Should the preaching of the gospel be banned on that account? Far from it! But if insurrection occurs, or if it is clear from a man's words or deeds that he wants to start one, whether it be among Christians, Anabaptists, Jews, or whatever faith it might be, then punish those who either engage in insurrection or seek to cause one by words or deeds. But as for the others, who simply follow their true or false faith and are peaceful, leave them undisturbed and let the word of God, the sceptre of the spiritual kingdom, rule and struggle among them.

Someone might say further: ought not one to punish before the insurrection actually appears, for if one waits until words or deeds indicate that an insurrection is brewing, it is already too late, for such sects meet in secret places and conceal their intentions, so that the rebellion has already broken out and is beyond control by the time one discovers the true nature of their actions. Answer: if an actual rebellion is not sufficient reason for eradicating the faith of those among whom it breaks out, as was demonstrated above, then a rebellion that has not yet happened but that one only fears is an even less sufficient ground for doing so. By far the greater number of the people in this world are evil and one must always fear the worst from them. Should one on that account kill or exile them all in order to assuage one's fear? No, God does not permit the secular government to do this, and the law also forbids that anyone be condemned or punished because of mere fear or suspicion. The secular government has been commanded to punish public crimes that it sees manifest in words and deeds, not secret matters or what someone contemplates doing. Indeed, this would be too difficult for the government, for it could never be certain and might be just as frightened of someone who had no evil in mind as of someone who did.

Moreover, the fact that some sects gather together in secret places is obviously not the fault of the sects or their members but of the government that will not tolerate them. Why do the secular authorities not leave faith to the spiritual realm and its king, Christ, and abandon their imprisonments, executions, and banishings on account of true or false belief? Then every sect would prefer to speak of its faith publicly and freely rather than secretly. Thereafter, if someone who had no cause to fear to speak openly of his faith nevertheless desired to practice it in secret, a government would have all the more right to forbid this and say to such a person: since you will not proclaim your faith openly so that one may test it to see if it is true, you must also leave off doing so in secret or else leave the country. But wherever public speech or teaching about faith is banned by the sword, people are thereby forced underground. As a result, there is added to the teaching of their faith the fact that the evil persons become hostile to the government that persecutes them and begin to plot moves designed to secure the free teaching of their doctrine, safe from persecution, so that the government thus to a certain extent causes and promotes secret conspiracy. It might well be argued that if anyone is certain of his faith and doctrine, he ought to bear witness to it in public and not conceal it, even though he were on that account executed. That is true and ought to be so. But not everyone is so perfect that he can die for the sake of his doctrine and faith, even though there are many whose consciences impel them not to remain silent in secret either. Indeed, we see every day that many of our people who adhere to the true faith teach people secretly and do not make much noise within earshot of the government when they find themselves in a place where their doctrine meets resistance. However, one must not despise the doctrine on account of their weak will but rather acknowledge it nevertheless to be true and have patience with the weak until they become stronger.

They are faint-hearted who fear that an uprising might suddenly prevail. For if a heathen government must rightfully be satisfied not to punish secret matters but only public crimes that it perceives through public deeds or learns of from adequate testimony, why should not a Christian government trust God to preserve it even though it violates neither justice nor the kingdom of Christ and punishes no one except those whose public crimes are known, and leaves the others, concerning whom it is not certain, in peace? For this is their consolation that whoever takes the sword (says Christ) shall perish by the sword.[11]

Now, insurgents always take the sword that no one has entrusted or commanded to them. Therefore God will surely smite and punish them by means of the other sword, namely that of the government, to whom he has commanded and entrusted it, as Solomon truly warns and says: "My son, fear the Lord and the king: and meddle not with them that are given to rebellion: For their calamity shall rise suddenly; and who knows the ruin of them both?"[12] And David says: "God will scatter the people that delight in war."[13] A government ought to rely on this and not be so fearful of such loose fellows, who are frightened even by a rustling leaf, that it lay violent hands on anyone or on their account violate the kingdom of Christ and thus also justice and good conscience.

Beyond this there is, in my opinion, only one other thing to recommend for the improvement of every government, whether it be heathen or Christian, namely that it perform its office, which is the maintenance of external peace, but with respect to true or false faith leave its sword sheathed and in matters of faith or sects confidently follow the advice of Gamaliel, Acts 5[:38–39]: "If this counsel or this work be of men, it will come to nothing: But if it be of God, you cannot overthrow it." And [let the government] say with the proconsul Gallio, Acts 18[:14–15]: "If it were a matter of wrong or wicked lewdness, I would hear you: But since it is a question of words and names, and of your law, look to it your-selves; for I will be no judge in such matters. And he drove them from the judgment seat." Or as Abraham answered and said to the rich man that his brothers had Moses and the prophets; if they would not hear them, neither would they be persuaded even if someone rose from the dead.[14] Similarly, a government should answer and say in the face of disunity over matters of faith: You

---

[11] Matt. 26:52.

[12] Prov. 24:21–22.

[13] Ps. 68:30.

[14] Luke 16:29–31.

have the word of God and his teachers and preachers; if you will not hear them, neither will you be persuaded even if I execute or banish a great number every day. What better thing could a government do than to do justice to the conscience of both and, beyond that, maintain external peace?

In our own day Doctor Martin Luther has given similar advice in his *Letter to the Saxon Princes Concerning the Rebellious Spirit*, where he says:[15] Since Paul writes that there must be sects in order that those who prove good may be made manifest,[16] one should confidently let the false spirits preach and let their spirit do battle with his.[17] If their spirit be true, it will have nothing to fear from his. On the other hand, if his be true, it will be preserved in the face of theirs. If in the process some are led astray, so be it. That is what happens in war; whenever there is a battle, some are killed or wounded, but whoever fights honourably will be crowned.[18] And he says further: But where the spirits go beyond this and not only fight with the word but also use their fists, whether it be he or the others, the government should not tolerate this but straightway forbid it and say: We will gladly see and suffer it that you spirits do battle with the word, in order that the true doctrine prove itself. But you must not use your fists, for that is our office. Otherwise clear out of our land!

Since, then, there must be sects and divisions in the kingdom of Christ, and since from them, though evil in themselves, something good will nevertheless result, why then should a government presume to use the sword to drive from Christ's kingdom something that scripture says must necessarily be in it? This would be nothing else than to contradict scripture and to want to make manifest in the spiritual realm the sword and its power rather than those who have proved good or the power of God's word.

But our Lord God knows a way to make us grasp that the sword cannot do the job. For it is well known what sort of a game the devil has played with the Anabaptists for the last two or three years, namely that the more the government has used its sword against

---

[15] Here the author paraphrases WA 15:218.19–219.4. Cf. AE 40:57–58.

[16] 1 Cor. 11:19.

[17] I.e., Luther's.

[18] 2 Tim. 2:5.

them, hanged or burned them, the more they have hastened to that very place and some have even surrendered themselves and said that even if the authorities wanted to imprison and execute them, they were prepared to suffer for their faith. In some places it has gotten so completely out of hand that the government, weary of executions, has had to desist.[19] It seems to me that this has made the sword dull in matters of faith and heresy and turned it into a fox's tail, so that the devil is laughing up his sleeve about it. And if God permits the devil to make his followers so joyous in the face of the sword, should not God give all the more power to his elect and true believers to triumph under his Christ against sword and fire, as the histories testify and as we have experienced in our own day? Thus, whether one uses the sword to execute true or false believers, in neither case is anything achieved except that the more that people see their fellows executed for their persecuted faith the more they are strengthened in it.

Since all of this is in fact so, why should a government make itself guilty of violating Christ's kingdom, which has not been entrusted to it, with injustice and tumult? And besides, will not all its hangings, care, and labour not only be in vain but also be sure to nourish and build up, all the more the longer they continue, the very thing they are intended to eradicate? Furthermore, if a Christian government forbids false faith, it thereby gives governments that adhere to false doctrine a pretext for combatting the true faith. For as soon as one admits that a government may impose penalties upon unbelievers, then every government will assume this right

------

[19] It is not clear what specific incidents, if any, the author has in mind. But in general it can be said that the years 1527 through 1533 were the bloodiest (679 executions, 352 in 1528–29 alone) in the history of Anabaptism in the area of Switzerland, south and central Germany, and the Austrian lands. While the councils of most imperial cities were extremely reluctant to impose the death penalty (Nürnberg, for example, executed only one Anabaptist; Schwäbisch Hall none), the governments of certain principalities, especially the Catholic princes of Bavaria and Austria, executed large numbers. Although it is probably true that most Anabaptists abandoned their faith in the face of persecution, it is equally true that the movement produced an astonishingly large number of individuals who faced imprisonment, torture, and death with remarkable courage. See Claus-Peter Clasen, *Anabaptism, A Social History, 1525–1618* (Ithaca and London: Cornell UP, 1972), chapter 11: "Persecution."

for itself—for none of them will admit to having a false faith—each one executing and banishing one after the other all those who are not of its faith.

And if one offers the excuse that the evangelical governments do not act so harshly but simply bar unbelievers from their lands, that is true; one penalty is more bearable than the other. But no matter how mild a penalty may be, it is nevertheless a penalty and it is thereby acknowledged that it is proper to penalize unbelief. And once the right to penalize is conceded, who will thereafter set limits to the harshness or mildness of the government's penalties against unbelief? And a Christian government will make itself an accomplice in the sins of others, which they could in good conscience have avoided becoming involved in.

For over a hundred years now there have been in the Kingdom of Bohemia Jews as well as three different [Christian] faiths,[20] and their kings have nevertheless maintained external peace and prevented tumult on account of religion.[21] Also, whoever has knowledge of history since the birth of Christ must admit, I think, that usually the emperors and governments who used their sword in matters of faith had far more unrest and tumult than the others, who did not do so but rather left the teaching of faith free to each individual. Why should it not also be possible today for a government to keep peace if it is otherwise diligently alert and watchful?

But if an insurrection should occur, one should not on that account despair. One must after all expect insurrections for far more trivial causes. But the government always has this consolation, as was shown above, that it will survive and that the rebels will fall and perish. As one saw in the peasants' rebellion, even though it occurred in many places because the governments would not tolerate the gospel. For this reason God indeed had ground to inflict a defeat upon them, as perhaps he may still do in due course. Nevertheless, he did not choose to do so by means of the rebellion of their subjects, though it seemed for a while that he did. Instead,

----

[20] Ordinary Catholics; Hussites, known as Calixtines or Utraquists; and the Bohemian Brethren (also known as the Unity of the Brethren), an offshoot of the Hussite movement.

[21] The tumults of the Hussite wars had disturbed the peace of Bohemia in the period 1420–34.

when things looked darkest, the tables were turned, the peasants were destroyed in their destroying and the governments escaped, so to speak, without so much as a broken leg. How much more gladly, then, will God help that government which keeps to its office and leaves Christ's kingdom unmolested. God grant that all governments may believe this. Amen. For otherwise the daily torture and execution of both true and false believers will not cease. And it is much to be feared that one day, precisely for the reason that one seeks to exterminate false belief by the sword, governments will come into conflict and whoever is the strongest will teach his doctrine to the others. Then there will be a real blood-letting, which the devil, as the signs already indicate, diligently seeks and promotes.

[Letter of the Anonymous Author to Spengler]

Dear Mr. Secretary, I would very much like to read the memorandum by...[22] though I do not have the time to do so today. But judging from your memorandum and from the note that you wrote me today,[23] you did not correctly understand me, or perhaps neither of us understood the other, in our recent war of words.[24] For it is not my opinion that a government should not have the power, in the faith to which it adheres, to conduct visitations, to appoint and dismiss preachers, and to establish ceremonies. Indeed, I say more: not only should a government have the power to do this with respect to its own faith, but so also should every group or sect in its own faith, so that Christians, Jews, Anabaptists, etc., all would be free to establish and observe without hindrance those doctrines and ceremonies which they regard as right and by which they hope to come to God, but in separate places, namely the Christians in their churches, the Anabaptists and Jews in their designated houses or synagogues.

I also say further that not only the government in its faith but also every sect—the Jews, Anabaptists, or others—should have the

---

[22] Blank space in the manuscript, where the name has been omitted.

[23] Neither the memorandum nor the note by Spengler is extant.

[24] A reference to the fact that the anonymous author and Spengler had had a long private discussion of their differences; see the first paragraph of Spengler's letter to Brenz, p. 37.

power to dismiss preachers or ministers whom they had appointed and subsequently found unfit for office, and to appoint others in their place, just as a government or community appoints and dismisses schoolteachers or shepherds.

But just as the Jews or Anabaptists may not tell a Christian secular government how it shall order its worship or whom it should have for teachers, so also the government should not forcibly impose preachers, ceremonies, or doctrines upon the Jews or Anabaptists.

This alone should be the government's office: if in its principality or territory anyone among the Jews, Christians, or Anabaptists resorts to force or crime, as for example if one party forcibly invades the synagogue or church of the other in order to establish its worship there, to attack the doctrines or disturb the ceremonies of the other, the government should not suffer this but administer penalties and restore peace.

Similarly, if a sect has dismissed a preacher or minister who nevertheless attempts to occupy and exercise his office[25] in the place from which he has been dismissed, or if a preacher attempts to preach where he does not have an appointment, then the government should, on the complaint of the injured group, step in and restore peace in such a way that every faith or sect, in such cases or in others that might arise, may have peace and quiet in its worship, doctrine, and ceremonies, as otherwise in secular affairs, just as hitherto peace was everywhere maintained for the Jews in their synagogues.

At the same time, the government should not prevent a preacher dismissed from one faith from being received into another, as for example from the Christian faith into the popish or Anabaptist faith. Nor should it prevent any of its subjects from going from one kind of worship to another in order to observe and learn, provided only that they not mock the doctrine and worship in any church or synagogue or cause any tumult or disorder, as hitherto Christians have visited Jewish synagogues.

----

[25] It is entirely possible that the correct translation of this passage should be "a preacher...who nevertheless attempts to exercise his office and collect his pay...." It depends on whether one reads "soldt einnemen" as "sollte einnehmen" (should occupy) or "Sold einnehmen" (collect pay).

Thus you have, along with the previous memorandum,[26] my full and complete opinion, unless Osiander's memorandum,[27] or one by you or someone else, has something new to say to me.

---

[26] I.e., the memorandum here translated.

[27] Cf. the first sentence of this letter, where the name of the author of one of the Nürnberg counter-memoranda was deliberately excised. The inclusion of Osiander's name here was undoubtedly an oversight on Spengler's part.

Document Number Three

An Answer to the Memorandum That Deals With This
Question: Whether Secular Government Has the
Right to Wield the Sword in Matters of Faith
[by Johannes Brenz, 8 May 1530]

First, it is true that the New Testament speaks of two kingdoms on
earth, namely a spiritual kingdom and a secular kingdom, etc.

Second, it is also true that each kingdom has its own distinct
king, sceptre, goal, and purpose, as the memorandum says.[1]

Third, it is also true that it is not appropriate for secular
government to protect true faith by force or by force to drive out
and punish false faith, etc.

But it is unacceptable that the author of the memorandum makes
no distinction between true or false faith on the one hand and the
works and deeds of true or false faith on the other. Indeed, he
mixes the two things together and concludes that because secular
government has no authority to punish false faith, it has no
authority to prevent or to punish the works or external deeds of
that false faith either. For this conclusion follows from his own
words where he maintains that every secular government is bound
in conscience to tolerate in its territory the public assembly of every
sect or faith, whether true or false, and at the same time to
guarantee peaceful conditions for them.[2]

But there is a great difference between these two things, true or
false faith on the one hand and public behaviour based on true or
false faith on the other, and if we carefully distinguish between the

---

[1] See pp. 42–3.
[2] See p. 53.

two and keep them separate, it will be clear what secular government may with good conscience prevent or hinder.

First of all, faith, whether true or false, is located in the heart. And since secular government is neither master nor lord of the human heart or conscience, it is in no way appropriate for government to undertake to punish or forcibly to prevent unbelief in the heart or conscience, as is known from the works of all the jurists.[3]

But then this same faith produces an external confession, which is done with the mouth. And this confession, as long as it remains personal and merely reveals and displays the heart and mind of a solitary individual, and as long as it is not used to teach others or cause them to band together, is not subject to the authority of secular government. On the contrary, like faith in the heart, personal confession with the mouth should also be free and secure from governmental authority. And both things are in fact matters of faith, which should not be subject to any worldly power. For even though confession with the mouth is an external, public act, it is nevertheless so integrated with the faith of the heart that both are counted as the same thing, and when one says that faith should be free, everyone understands this to include the confession of that same faith.

But when it does not remain a matter of faith in the heart and confession with the mouth but rather goes to the point that people band together, whether in public or in private, and establish and begin a new teaching office, then it begins to be appropriate for secular government to intervene in such actions, and, if the assembly and teaching office appear to be useful and peaceful, to promote them, or, if there be good grounds for judging them to be damaging and unpeaceful, to check them.

And this I shall prove with the help of God: first from the Old Testament, and second, after having shown that the Old Testament is useful to the New, out of the New Testament. Third, [I shall prove this] with the words and opinions of the author of the memorandum himself, and also with other demonstrable reasons based on common sense.

------

[3] An apparent reference to the legal maxim that thoughts are not indictable.

[First.] In the thirteenth chapter of the book of Deuteronomy[4] it is written: "If a prophet or a dreamer arises among you and gives you a sign" etc. "and says: Let us go after other gods and serve them," etc., "that prophet shall be put to death, so that you purge the evil from the midst of you."

In this decree it must be noticed first of all that it is not false faith or the mere personal confession of it that is abolished or punished but rather the teaching or preaching office, for the law does not say: Whoever believes falsely, but rather: "When a prophet says: Let us go after other gods." So among the Jews, too, false faith went unpunished and only the teaching or preaching office of a false faith was stopped.

In the second place, it is clear that among the Jews the administration and execution of this law was assigned to the kings, i.e., to the secular government. For when the Jews chose and anointed a king, the Levites placed into his hands a copy of this book of Deuteronomy, which contains the above-mentioned law, so that he might rule his kingdom according to its teachings and statutes.[5]

But it is said that the Old Testament no longer binds anyone and that if one is bound by one provision, one cannot avoid being bound by the others.[6] It is true and certain that the Old Testament in and of itself no longer binds or constrains anyone. Nevertheless, as Paul testifies in 2 Tim. 3[:16], "all scripture" of the Old Testament "is given by inspiration of God, and is profitable for teaching, for reproof, for correction, and for training in righteousness," etc. Paul himself uses many passages from the Old Testament for purposes of teaching, namely in 1 Cor. 9[:1–12], where he teaches that the apostles should be provided with food and drink and that they, the apostles, by virtue of their office, have a right to food and drink, and cites as his authority the law of Moses, Deuteronomy 25[:4]: "You shall not muzzle an ox when it treads out the grain." Might not someone have confronted Paul and said: My dear fellow, the Old Testament binds Christians not at all, as you yourself have preached, so your text proves nothing. Paul would certainly have

---

[4] Verses 1, 2, 5.

[5] See Deuteronomy 17:18–20.

[6] See p. 42.

replied as follows: I know very well that the letter of the Old Testament binds no one, but no one can on that account forbid me to cite something from it for purposes of doctrine and instruction. He does the same thing in 2 Cor. 13[:1], where he says: "This is the third time I am coming to you; in the mouth of two or three witnesses must everything be established." Is this regulation not taken from Deuteronomy, chapter 17[:6]?[7] Thus it is indeed true that the letter of the above-cited law about putting false prophets to death no longer binds any Christian government. On the other hand, because it was the case that among the Jews the execution of this law was assigned by divine ordinance to the secular magistrate, it follows that today one may properly extract from this a lesson for the Christian magistrate concerning his office, namely that he should seek just and appropriate means to curb false and damaging doctrine and worship among his subjects. Similarly, a preacher of the truth should draw from the same passage the lesson that it also behooves him, for himself and in his own way, to confront and curb false preaching among the people of his parish. And thus we have here instruction for both offices, for the secular magistrate and the preacher, each in its own appropriate way, the secular government with its secular penalties or restraints, and the preacher with his spiritual penalties and restraints.

But again it is said:[8] A secular government could well draw from this law[9] the lesson that it would be justified in putting a false teacher to death rather than just expelling him from office or from the territory. What would be the outcome of that? Answer: The government cannot do this; for if it were to insist on the letter of the law in this instance, then it would be bound by all the other laws of Moses, as is correctly stated in the memorandum on the basis of St. Paul in Galatians 5[:3].[10] To avoid error, the government must draw its lesson from the intent and purpose of this law, which is ultimately that evil and disorder should be prevented. Can a government do that with fair words? In all likelihood it will only be able to do so by means of banishment from the territory, but

---

[7] It seems, in fact, to come more directly from Deut. 19:15.

[8] See p. 42.

[9] I.e., Deuteronomy 13:1–2, 5.

[10] See p. 42.

surely only after all convenient, godly means to curb evil and disorder have been tried by the government. If evil and disorder are and can be prevented, by whatever means, without the penalty of bodily death, then that is enough to satisfy the intent and purpose of the law.

Second, there is proof of this in the New Testament,[11] namely in St. Paul, 1 Tim. 2[:1–2]: "I exhort," says Paul, "that first of all intercessions be made for kings and all governments, so that we may lead a quiet and peaceable life." Observe that it is incumbent on government to maintain a quiet and peaceable life among Christians. Now there is nothing that makes Christians more agitated and disquieted than the emergence among them of false preachers and separate sects. We are told that if two people were to quarrel and wrangle with one another over two cents, the government should intervene but that if, on the other hand, they were to quarrel with one another publicly from the pulpit over doctrinal matters and were not to keep it a matter of personal disagreement but were rather to awaken disquiet and confusion in the congregation, that the government should not intervene and restore peace by convenient, untyrannical means. It is true that the government cannot step in as a judge of doctrines, but it should step in as the judge of disorder and disunity, because it pertains to its office to maintain a quiet and peaceable life among its subjects.

Moreover, this is proved by the words of the author of the memorandum himself, for he writes as follows: "The secular government has been commanded to punish public crimes that it sees manifest in words and deeds" etc.[12] But is it not a public crime if ten or twenty citizens in a town (where perhaps one or two thousand live) are peaceful members of the church and are content with the preacher that has been properly appointed by their government but then, over a period of four or six weeks, separate themselves and try to establish their own assembly and even, contrary to the order established by their government, to inaugu-

---

[11] Here Brenz is not simply continuing the thought of the previous paragraph but rather commencing the second part of the tripartite argument outlined in paragraph 4 on p. 56.

[12] See p. 46.

rate a new preaching office? If they do not like the preacher who has been properly appointed by the government, they can still believe what they wish or move away. But to go beyond their personally chosen faith and to establish a new assembly and preaching office in a community that is not theirs to govern and in which they have no public authority, that is a public crime. And when the government intervenes, one cannot accuse it of attempting to control faith. Let everyone believe and confess for himself whatever he wishes, that is certainly no concern of the secular magistrate; but it does concern the magistrate when someone establishes a new sect[13] or a new preaching office without its permission.

Here someone might object and say:[14] By this rule, the apostles should not have preached until they had been either called by the government or granted its permission. But since in fact they preached without the warrant of the government, often indeed contrary to governmental ban, they must, according to what was said above, have done wrong. Answer: It is certainly true, beyond question or doubt, that the apostles acted contrary to governmental ordinances. But one must ask whether their behaviour contrary to governmental fiat constituted a punishable crime. To be sure, if one chooses to judge the matter according to external appearances, it is a crime, and it was proper for a pagan or a Jewish government, according to its pagan or Jewish faith, to examine the case. I do not say that it was proper for them to have a pagan or a Jewish faith. Indeed, the most appropriate course would have been for

---

[13] Sometimes, as in the fourth paragraph of this memorandum (p. 55) and again in the last paragraph (p. 72), Brenz uses the German word "sect," the meaning of which is exactly rendered by the cognate English term. But here and in several other passages he uses the word "rotirung," which is related to the verb "sich rotten" (to band together, usually for nefarious purposes). By so doing, he deliberately implies that those who form new sects are unruly and potentially dangerous people. These overtones of disorder and rebelliousness are not adequately conveyed by the word "sect." On the other hand, if "sect" says too little, the standard English equivalents of "rotirung" (mob, gang, horde, rabble, etc.) all say too much and make Brenz's rhetoric sound more lurid than it actually is. Thus, for want of a better term, "rotirung" has in all instances been translated as "sect."

[14] Cf. pp. 43, paragraph 1, and 46, lines 7–11.

them to inquire into the true faith, acquire it, and adhere to it. But since they had always been of the Jewish or pagan faith, they did not do as they should have. But according to their faith they acted conscientiously and prudently when they took action against a new sect or preaching office established contrary to their faith. And I deem it a foolish and imprudent government, whatever faith it may adhere to, that heedlessly allows a new assembly contrary to its faith to arise among its subjects. But if it desires to act justly as well as prudently, it must first of all take the true faith to heart and then, so far as is appropriate to its office, promote that faith and keep it peaceful.

Now, with respect to the conduct of the apostles, it is true that they committed a crime against the government. But not every crime is sinful and punishable. Just as Moses and Phinehas committed murder but were not liable to punishment for it,[15] so the crime of the apostles was no sin, because they had been called to it by God and could publicly certify and prove their call with miracles, as though with letter and seal, to both Jews and pagans. So now, if a sect or preaching office springs up in some town or other outside the common order and contrary to governmental prohibition and those responsible want to establish their right to commit such a crime, then they are obliged to do so by performing public miracles. If they do not do that, then one is justified in judging their crime to be sinful and punishable.

But again someone might say: According to this rule the evangelical preachers committed a crime because they did not confirm their teaching with miracles. Answer: I am not speaking here of the doctrine, whatever its merits might be, but of the public teaching office and of the public or secret sect. Now, because the evangelical preachers have been duly called by the government and perform their calling and office in those places to which the government has summoned them and where the secular government permits an assembly, no one can accuse them of any crime and they do not need to perform any miracles, since they assumed their office lawfully. But they must take care that they are able to render account for their teaching. Just as a secular official who has been appointed to his office by the government does not need to

---

[15] Exod. 2:11–15, Num. 25:7–13.

account for his call to that office, for he was lawfully called to it (and the government knows that), but must render account for his conduct in office, so is it in the case of a preacher who has been duly called by the government.

But anyone who has unlawfully entered the preaching office must render account not only for his teaching but also for his call. If he cannot do this, he is guilty of a crime. And indeed, recent experience should have been sufficient to teach us that unlawful preaching, even if some truth be mixed in with it, leads to no good. When both peasants and scholars began some years ago to preach without call or appointment, that brought us the drama of the Peasants' Revolt.

And our memorandist admits this in his second memorandum,[16] where he says: "If a preacher attempts to preach where he does not have an appointment, then the government should restore peace" etc. Suppose then that in some place where there are no Anabaptists and no preacher, a few citizens adopt the Anabaptist faith and choose a preacher from among their number, who would say that this preacher had been lawfully called? For individual citizens or subjects have no authority to call a preacher; or if they have such authority, it is proper that they supply proof of it. But if they cannot publicly certify their authority, should not the lawful government have the power to curb their crime? If it has the power to prevent the formation of guilds where none exist, must it not also have the power to prevent the formation of a new religious group in its territory?

We are asked to accept[17] that if it were to happen that in the space of one week an entire neighbourhood of people living in one particular street in a city converted from Christianity to Judaism and had themselves circumcised according to Jewish custom, the government would be obliged to allow them to build their own synagogue and to grant them the right to do everything according to the law of Moses. Who would be so mad as to recommend any such thing to a government?

It is another matter when subjects who adhere to two or three faiths accept and confirm government on the condition that it

---

[16] I.e., in his letter to Spengler; see p. 53.
[17] See p. 52.

permit everyone the observance of his own religion, as the Jews accepted the Romans, and the Bohemians, so they say, accepted Ferdinand.[18] Similarly, Joshua promised security to the Gibeonites and had to keep his word even though the Israelites had otherwise been commanded to extirpate all alien religions in the land of Canaan.[19] However, as for allowing a new sect or teaching office to enter its territory, a government may well have reasons for doing so, as perhaps the authorities in Worms and Frankfurt have good grounds for tolerating the Jews.[20] But I can find no reason why a government should be forced or compelled by virtue of its office to do any such thing, etc.

And in the ancient histories it is recorded that some emperors tolerated heretics alongside the catholics. But it is also recorded that the Christian emperors who had always adhered to Christianity tolerated no heretical churches. Thus it is written in the *Historia Tripartita*,[21] book 3, chapter 11 [1f.]: "The doctrine of Arius, although many had exalted it in disputations, nevertheless did not yet mark off a separate group that was known by the name of its founder, but rather all came together in the churches and took part there except for the Novitians and those who were called Phrygians

---

[18] In October 1526, Archduke Ferdinand of Austria was elected King of Bohemia after having agreed to uphold the rights of the Estates, which included the right to adhere to any of several legally recognized religions. See p. 51, note 20.

[19] Josh. 9.

[20] By 1530, Frankfurt am Main and Worms were in fact the only imperial cities that still tolerated Jews. The Jewish communities that had existed in other imperial cities had been eliminated in the great wave of pogroms and expulsions that filled the period from the Black Death in the middle of the fourteenth century down to the eve of the Reformation. The Jews of Nürnberg had been expelled in 1499. Those in most of the larger princely territories had been expelled as well. The few surviving communities lived in fear that their turn for expulsion might be next. See Salo Wittmayer Baron, *A Social and Religious History of the Jews* 11 (New York and London: Columbia UP, 1967):271–83.

[21] The *Historica Ecclesiastica Tripartita*, compiled from the works of the Greek church historians Theodoretus, Socrates, and Sozomenus and translated into Latin at the instigation of the sixth-century Roman writer Cassiodorus. It covers the period A.D. 306–439.

and the Valentinians and the Marcionites and the Paulianists and whoever practised other heresies. Against all of these the emperor issued a decree commanding that their houses of prayer be taken from them, that they be forced into the churches, and that they hold no assemblies either in private houses or in public" etc. Again, in the same *Historia*, book 9, chapter 7 [2f.]: "Emperors Gratian, Valentinian, and Theodosius to the people of the city of Constantinople. It is our will that all the peoples who live under our gracious rule abide in that religion" etc.[22] Justinian included this mandate in his Codex under the title "Concerning the Most High Trinity and the Catholic Faith."[23] A parallel example of an imperial mandate is recorded in the same *Historia Tripartita*, book 9, chapter 10, and again in book 9, chapter 19 [16]: "The emperor decreed that the heretics were neither to have churches nor to teach concerning their faith nor to ordain bishops or others. Some of them were driven from the cities while others he allowed to remain there without honour or the benefits of citizenship. Moreover, he included in the same decree some cruel punishments against them which, however, were not enforced. For his aim was to move them to unity [with the orthodox] rather than to inflict suffering" etc. In the same book, chapter 25 [5]: "Hearing this, the emperor, amazed at his words and deeds, hastily published a law whereby the councils of the heretics were forbidden" etc. From this it is clear that the pious emperors intervened at various times in the assemblies of the heretics and forbade them. And, as far as I am aware, they were not on that account denounced as godless by any pious bishop, which would certainly have happened if the bishops had deemed their behaviour unjust and beyond the authority of secular government.

I must also briefly answer some of the claims and objections of the author of the memorandum. First of all, he says the following: "Nowhere does one find that the apostles, if someone did not adhere to their doctrine and preaching but rather believed or taught some other faith, appealed to the secular government" etc.[24] It is

---

[22] The text goes on to specify "that religion" which is orthodox on the subject of the trinity.

[23] *Corpus juris civilis, Codex Iustinianus* 1.1.

[24] See p. 43.

true that the apostles did not invoke the secular government against those who believed falsely. Nor does any Christian preacher do so. I will go even further: the apostles never invoked a secular government against a thief or a murderer, and no true preacher does so either. But does it then follow that a true preacher may not advise the government concerning its office and, if it should come to that, instruct the government that it may with good conscience punish thieves and murderers and that it is indeed obligated to do so? Therefore, if it happens that a Christian government for conscience' sake asks the preachers if it may with good conscience abolish in its territory the self-constituted assemblies and the self-appointed preachers of a competing faith, should it be tantamount to invoking the government if a preacher so asked instructs and teaches the government concerning its office? Paul teaches concerning government that is ordained of God to punish the wicked[25] and to enable its subjects to lead a quiet and peaceable life.[26] Should he on that account be accused of invoking the government against his opponents, who day and night sought to kill him? Far be it! Accordingly, there is a great difference between these two things: instructing a government concerning its office and petitioning or calling on the government for help and deliverance. The former pertains to all preachers, the latter to all subjects in dire, secular need.

To argue that one does not find in the New Testament that any secular government was praised on that account[27] is pointless, for the argument from silence is invalid. Besides, neither does one find that any government was denounced for having refused to tolerate the assembly of a false faith. Moreover, at the time when the New Testament was written, governments were not Christian, so that no one could either praise or blame them on this account in any case.

Next, although Christ says in Matthew 13[:29–30] that one should not pull up the tares but let them grow, etc.,[28] that does not mean that one should remain quiet or do nothing but rather that in this passage Christ has set a limit to the apostolic office. He saw and

---

[25] Rom. 13:4.

[26] 1 Tim. 2:2.

[27] See p. 43.

[28] Ibid.

noticed that his apostles were too inclined to resort to sword and fist, as was apparent in Luke 9[:54], when they wanted him to call down fire from heaven to consume the Samaritans, and also when Peter resisted with the sword while Christ was being taken prisoner.[29] Therefore he teaches them that their office does not extend to the use of the secular sword. Nevertheless, it is fitting that they should pull up the tares in manner appropriate to their office, for if it were not so, then no preacher could preach against heresy, and Paul would have behaved unjustly when he wrote against the circumcisers and other heretics. But does not writing or preaching against false faith or teaching constitute pulling up tares? It most certainly does! Just as it is fitting for a preacher to act according to the precepts of his calling, that is, by using the word of God, so it is also fitting for a secular government to do the same according to the principles of its office, i.e., each office does as befits it. Otherwise, according to this passage no secular government would be entitled to punish robbers, murderers, or blasphemers. Is not murder a tare? Are not blasphemy and public cursing tares? Is not adultery a tare? I gather then [from the memorandist's reading of the text] that the government would have to permit these tares to grow until the harvest and could not punish anyone for them. Consequently, Christ in this passage forbids the apostles to employ force in the conduct of their office, but at the same time leaves each office, both the spiritual and the secular, free to act according to the precepts and principles of its mandate and, to the extent possible, to pull up the tares.

It is indeed written that Christ will do battle in his kingdom.[30] But if this is to be understood to mean that no one should do anything about the tares, then the preachers could preach nothing against them and ordinary Christians could not pray or cry out to God against them. But Christ does battle particularly when preachers cry out and Christians pray against the tares.

It is also written that almighty God rules in heaven and on earth. I suppose that one might conclude from this that secular government has no right to rule. That would be splendid logic! The truth is that when the preachers combat lies with the word of God and the

---

[29] Matt. 26:51.

[30] Isa. 11:4 as interpreted in the anonymous memorandum; see pp. 43–4.

secular government employs suitable means to combat all disorder, immorality, and dissension, then one can truly say that especially then Christ is doing battle and that almighty God is ruling through the preachers and the government as his appointed instruments.

It is true that Daniel says that the Antichrist will be destroyed "without hand."[31] But does he also write that therefore a Christian government must allow Antichrist's preaching or assembly to enter or move into its territory? No, he writes no such thing. So if a secular government refuses to permit any new preaching office or false faith to enter its territory, it does [not] thereby venture to destroy the Antichrist; it ventures, rather, to maintain quiet, peaceable, and harmonious conduct[32] among its subjects.

The Jews are also a part of the Antichrist. And because the Antichrist will be destroyed without hand, we are told that secular governments everywhere must admit the Jews and permit them to establish their synagogues and preaching office.[33] But who would wish to compel them to do that? It is true that to take in the Jews is a work of mercy, but to grant them their own synagogue and teaching office, that is something that no one can impose or press upon the conscience of any government.

And further, it is true that certain words of Christ—those that he uttered to the man who asked him to make his brother divide an inheritance with him, and also those spoken to his disciples and to Pilate—prove that the two kingdoms must be distinguished.[34] However, for the reasons cited above, one cannot conclude from this that a secular government must permit Sacramentarians,[35] Anabaptists, Jews, Turks, or others of that nature to enter its territory and establish, among subjects living in external unity of faith, a new assembly and teaching office.

Moreover, a secular government must curb not only those things that by their nature cause tumult but also those that cause public scandal and offence. For example: to take two or three wives causes no tumult, as one can see among the Turks, who have many

---

[31] Dan. 8:25; see p. 44.

[32] Cf. 1 Tim. 2:2.

[33] See p. 52.

[34] Luke 12:13–14, John 18:36, Luke 22:25–26; see p. 44.

[35] I.e., Zwinglians.

wives, and as we know from the Jews, who before the advent of Christ also had many wives. Should a government on that account not punish someone who takes two or three wives? And cursing: "[God's] power and strength," "Valentine and wounds,"[36] as it is the custom to swear, these bring no public tumult either; should they on that account not be punished by the government? Therefore, even though the teaching office and the assembly of a false faith bring no tumult, they nevertheless cause confusion and disorder, as well as a discordant spirit, among Christians. Therefore, *quod non possit illorum affectus esse fidus quorum diversa est fides,*[37] why should the government not be entitled to intervene in the matter?

The author of the memorandum believes that it would be appropriate for a secular government confidently to follow the advice of Gamaliel, who in Acts 5[:38–39] says: "If this undertaking is of men, it will fail; but if it is of God, you cannot overthrow it" etc.[38] That would perhaps be good, prudent, rational advice for a government that did not know which pot the barley was in and what the true and best faith was, and that also wanted to proceed too tyrannically. This was the case when Gamaliel spoke these words, for the scribes, overcome by the great miracles of the apostles, were filled with self-doubt and wanted only to slay and hang them.[39] But in the case of a Christian government that has a faith well grounded in holy scripture, this would be dubious advice and would awaken the impression that it still vacillated in faith and was at loose ends.

Nor does the speech of Gallio in Acts 18[:14–15] serve any purpose here,[40] for as a heathen, Gallio had taken office on the condition that he respect the legal rights of the Jews. Since it is fitting that one do as one has promised, it follows that he acted

---

[36] I.e., "May St. Valentine's plague [epilepsy] and [also] wounds befall you!"

[37] "Because those who are divided in faith cannot have a faithful spirit." Paraphrase of a passage in Jerome, *Commentarium in Mattheum* 1, on Matt. 10:21; *Corpus Christianorum, Series Latina* 77 (Turnholt: Typographi Brepols, 1969):69, lines 1658–60. Thanks are due to Erika Rummel for supplying this reference.

[38] See p. 48.

[39] Acts 4:13–16, 5:12–33.

[40] Cf. p. 48.

prudently when in conformity with his accepted obligation he refused to exercise jurisdiction over the faith or the religious disputes of the Jews. But according to the author of the memorandum, Gallio must have acted imprudently, for in his second memorandum[41] he says the following: "If a sect has dismissed a preacher or minister who nevertheless attempts to occupy and exercise his office in the place from which he has been dismissed, or if a preacher attempts to preach where he does not have an appointment, then the government should, on the complaint of the injured group, step in and restore peace" etc. Those are his words. But in Achaia the Jews had not called Paul as a preacher and for that reason they lodged a complaint against him with the government, as is reported in Acts 18[:12ff.]. But the proconsul, Gallio, refused to deal with the case or the complaint. According to our memorandist, he must thereby have behaved imprudently.

But it has already been said[42] that it is one thing to permit entry to a new sect and quite another to condescend to maintain an old, well-established sect in external peace and grant it the exercise of its ancient rights and traditions, etc.

As for Abraham's reply to the rich man: "You have Moses and the prophets" etc.,[43] a government can cite this against those who in private believe and personally confess a false faith, and it can also cite it against those who, contrary to its ban, begin a new sect and teaching office, namely as follows: We do not intend to punish you on account of your false faith and personal confession, for you have God's word as well as his teachers and preachers. If you refuse to hear them, our punishment will not help you in any way. But because you are presuming, without our command, to assemble with other people, and without our call to establish new preaching offices, we do on that account intend to punish you, etc.

The memorandist also says: "If a Christian government forbids false faith, it thereby gives governments that adhere to false doctrine a pretext for combatting the true faith" etc.[44] The answer

---

[41] I.e., in the letter to Spengler; see p. 53.

[42] See pp. 62–3.

[43] Luke 16:29–31; cf. p. 48.

[44] See pp. 50–1.

to this, as indicated above,[45] is that here again no distinction is made between faith and the external works of faith, and also that it is true that no Christian government should curb a false faith or confession. But, as was said above,[46] it may curb the assembly and the new public offices [of a false faith], and falsely believing governments are not thereby given leave to do injustice.

For it is entirely within the discretion of a government, whether it be of true or false faith, either to tolerate or to curb a new association, guild, or sect in its territory, entirely according to its good judgment, and it is under no constraint either way. If a government has a false faith and will not permit the assembly of true believers in its territory, that is, properly considered, wrong, as was in part indicated above.[47] But by the standards of its false faith, such a government acts not imprudently or unjustly. They have zeal, but without knowledge, as Paul says.[48] Indeed, I would deem it a dissolute, wicked, and indolent government that, faced with something that it in good conscience regarded as unjust and detrimental to its subjects, did not make every possible effort to curb the injustice. Such a government would certainly no more be forgiven by God for that than was Brennus, duke of the Gauls, forgiven by God when his troops reviled and insulted Apollo, who was really only an idol but was deemed by them to be a real god, and robbed his temple.[49] For God wants to be feared for his name's sake even among idolaters and he also wants to be feared in a false faith, and it is extremely blameworthy to act against one's conscience, dissolutely or wickedly, in either a true or a false faith.

And finally, even though, as the memorandist reminds us, there must be sects and divisions in the kingdom of Christ,[50] it does not

---

[45] See p. 55.

[46] See p. 56.

[47] See pp. 60–1.

[48] Rom. 10:2.

[49] Brennus was the leader of a body of Gauls that had settled in Pannonia. Invading Greece in 279 B.C., he eventually set about the plunder of Delphi. His barbarian soldiers mocked the gods on the sacred hill, but their assault on the temple was frustrated by the skill of the defenders and also by a violent winter storm, which Greek and Roman historians attributed to the intervention of Apollo. Disgraced and wounded, Brennus committed suicide.

[50] 1 Cor. 11:19; see p. 49.

follow from this that one should not curb sects and divisions to the extent that it is possible and appropriate for each office. Were there not sects at Corinth, and were there not divisions there as well? But see how dauntlessly Paul resists them and how vehemently he scolds the Corinthians on that account.[51] But if sects and divisions absolutely must exist, then no one need resist them, neither preacher nor apostle. And where the memorandist says: "Why should a government presume to use the sword to drive from Christ's kingdom something that scripture says must necessarily be in it,"[52] one could just as well say in almost the same words: Why should a preacher presume to use the preached word to drive from Christ's kingdom something that scripture says must necessarily be in it, etc.?

But this verse of St. Paul[53] is so to be understood that the mandate of the two offices, spiritual and secular, is not abrogated by it. Indeed, whoever is able to do so should resist sects and divisions: "Blessed are the peacemakers, for they shall be called the children of God."[54] Paul's intent in this verse[55] is to show what results from the devil's regime. For because the devil is the prince of this world[56] and goes about like a roaring lion, seeking someone to devour,[57] there must be quarrels and dissensions, in worldly matters as well as in those of faith, just as many are called but few are chosen.[58] The result is that those who are peaceful and righteous will be made known.[59] Thus, it is neither just nor godly but rather forbidden by God to live in a quarrelsome and contentious way, even though the devil is still to some extent in power and such things must be, and even though the nature of the world is such that there must always be much evil. Nevertheless, it is the duty of a preacher to combat sects with the word of God. And it is the duty of secular government to prevent all public disorder

---

[51] 1 Cor. 1:10–13.

[52] See p. 49.

[53] I.e., 1 Cor. 11:19.

[54] Matt. 5:9.

[55] I.e., in 1 Cor. 11:19.

[56] Cf. John 16:11.

[57] 1 Pet. 5:8.

[58] Matt. 20:16 (ASV).

[59] 1 Cor. 11:19.

and confusion, and it is not bound in conscience to permit the establishment of a new sect, synagogue, or public assembly to the detriment of true Christians, but may in good conscience resist the harmful undertaking of the new sect and abolish it by appropriate, moderate, untyrannical means etc.

Document Number Four

Whether a Secular Government May Regulate Spiritual Matters, Restrain False Teaching, and Put Down Ungodly Abuses
[Andreas Osiander or Wenzeslaus Linck, before 26 March 1530]

An Admonition to Avoid Unnecessary and Vain Questions and Disputes, Since Such Things Produce Nothing But Confusion and Deception

The more dangerous the times are and the more Satan rages, the more the difficult and unnecessary questions that make their appearance. Thus we read that at the time of our Lord Jesus Christ and his beloved apostles, when the gospel was at flood tide and had immense power, Satan moved and swayed the people with many questions and disputes on all sorts of matters affecting both spiritual and secular government. For it is his custom, by means of such unnecessary, indeed foolish, questions to distract men from necessary and wholesome matters (for he can invent a thousand tricks) and to lead them away from the simple path of truth. Such vain, useless questions are also often a sign of an unbelieving, vacillating, unstable conscience, as is often the case in the gospel with the Pharisees and others who tempted Christ; for by such questions God is commonly tempted or mocked and not honoured.[1] Wherefore Christ, our Lord God and Saviour, faithfully warns us that we should "beware of the leaven of the Pharisees

---

[1] See Matt. 16:1, 22:18, 35; Luke 10:25.

and Saducees."[2] For these same people thought themselves clever and treated of their religion by means of strange, subtle questions and disputations, just as our scholastic theologians deal by means of subtle disputations with all those matters that should be grasped in the simplest way and with simple faith. Thus one not inappropriately says: *Quod firmiter credit iurista catholicus, ho[c] in dubium vertit perfidus aut perversus theologus.*[3]

Paul admonishes and warns us in a similar way when he says to Timothy: "Have nothing to do with foolish frivolous controversies, for you know that they only breed quarrels. But a servant of the Lord must not be quarrelsome."[4] Here he indicates two kinds of harmful questions. The first are foolish, serving only human reason or cleverness and not the faith that leads to improvement, for in the scriptures he who is godless and without faith is called a fool, no matter how clever or wise he otherwise may be.[5] The other questions, though not directly contrary to faith and godless, are nevertheless frivolous, that is, without discipline or the improvement of morals, or at least are less conducive to humility than to the arrogance that produces vain disputes. Everyone is determined to have the last word and dominate the others, as it is written: "Among the haughty there is always strife."[6] Thus they never arrive at the truth, as is clear in the case of our scholastic theologians, who are "ever learning and can never come to the knowledge of the truth,"[7] "but those who take advice are wise."[8]

Accordingly, Paul commands his disciple Titus to strive "that those who have believed in God may be careful to apply themselves to good deeds; these are excellent and profitable to men. But avoid stupid controversies, genealogies, dissensions, and quarrels over the law, for they are unprofitable and futile."[9] Similarly he writes to Timothy: "As I urged you, remain at Ephesus that you

---

[2] Matt. 16:6.

[3] "Whatever a catholic jurist firmly believes, some faithless or perverse theologian will turn to doubt." The source of this saying is unidentified.

[4] 2 Tim. 2:23–24.

[5] See Ps. 14:1; Luke 24:25; 1 Cor. 1:18–25, 2:14, 3:19.

[6] Prov. 13:10, Vulgate.

[7] 2 Tim. 3:7.

[8] Prov. 13:10.

[9] Tit. 3:8–9.

may charge certain persons not to teach anyone different doctrine, nor to occupy themselves with myths and endless genealogies which promote speculations rather than divine training that is in faith."[10] These and similar warnings of the Holy Spirit ought properly to cause us to abstain from numerous questions and disputations, because we know that God takes no pleasure in them and that no profit or well-being accrues to us from them, and that because they flow not from the spirit of God but rather from our own arrogance and boastfulness, as Solomon says: "I have found that God has made man upright, but they seek much knowledge" and embroil themselves in many questions. "Who is so wise and who can interpret these things?"[11] With their own learning, disputations, questions, or inventions men destroy themselves and fall away from the image of God in which they were created,[12] which the disputation between Eve and the serpent sufficiently demonstrates.[13]

Therefore, every pious Christian would be well advised to beware of the proliferation of questions, even though those questions touch God's law, lest he be deceived by the cunning tricks of the serpent and led astray from the simplicity that is in Christ.[14] For just as one fool usually makes a second, so one question always begets others. Whoever does not want to follow my advice, but thinks himself wise, let him pose questions as long as he pleases and let him see whether he does not become more perplexed the longer he does so. Pursuing impertinent questions is like getting lost in the woods: the longer one continues, the more lost one becomes; only by chance does one manage to find the way out.

Nonetheless, it often happens that pious men who believe in Christ become entangled in difficult questions; for no one is so wise that he does not make a fool of himself now and then. Therefore, one must be patient with such people and deal with their questions as best one can.

---

[10] 1 Tim. 1:3–4.

[11] Eccl. 7:29, 8:1.

[12] Gen. 1:27.

[13] Gen. 3:1–4.

[14] 2 Cor. 11:3.

Just as at the time of Christ many questions arose concerning secular government between the emperor's [...][15] and similar things under the title of Christian freedom,[16] it also happens in our time that many pious people, perhaps because of the old invented custom of the clerical estate (which the papists have exempted from secular jurisdiction and completely separated from the secular sphere, like the sun from the moon, or heaven from earth, and, because of their greed and luxury, shamefully duped the secular estate), worry whether secular government has the authority to do or command anything in spiritual matters, such as errors or dissensions in matters of faith, false preaching, unchristian, self-contrived worship, misuse of religion, etc.

Whether a Secular Government May Regulate Spiritual Matters, Restrain False Teaching, and Put Down Ungodly Abuses

In the case of such questions it is Satan's custom adroitly and masterfully to introduce false teaching and thus bring things to the point that one does not proceed on the certain ground of scripture but rather forces scripture down a false path. We want to demonstrate that such is the case here.

First of all, there are two kingdoms: of God and of the world, or spiritual and temporal. Some want to separate these so completely from one another that neither should have any dealings with the other, etc.[17] Here they have already gone off the track, for it is well known that the spiritual realm, which exists in faith and the word of God, often turns to the temporal realm and lays down laws for its conduct. Christ teaches and indeed commands that one should love God above all things and one's neighbour as one's self,[18] that we should live with one another without evil desires, anger, envy, etc., that each should help, counsel, serve and love the other, etc., all of which things the secular realm has the duty

---

[15] Here the copyist clearly left something out.

[16] See Matt. 17:24–27, 22:15–21.

[17] This is directed against the author of the anonymous memorandum; see pp. 42–5.

[18] Matt. 22:37–40.

to promote and, as far as possible, to enforce. On the other hand, one should deal with all secular or temporal matters in faith and in spirit, so that these two realms are not separated from one another but rather constantly serve one another, just as one hand serves the other. For if one were to separate them, one would ultimately also have to divide and separate the divinity of Christ from his humanity as well as the body of a man from his soul or spirit. Therefore, it is completely off the track to say that someone belonging to the spiritual realm may not or should not deal with matters of the secular realm whenever necessity or love requires, and vice-versa.

But though Christ and the apostles acted only with the word of God, exercising spiritual government and refraining entirely from temporal government,[19] it does not follow that they could not have wielded the sword if they had been called to do so or if necessity and love had required it. Their example proves nothing more than that everyone should remain in his own calling[20] and not wantonly meddle in matters pertaining to other callings. As St. Paul too teaches, when he says: "No soldier on service gets involved in civilian pursuits," etc.[21] But he does not thereby forbid or condemn civilian pursuits. Moreover, Christ and the apostles not only inculcated faith by the word but also struggled against those who contradicted it, as St. Paul says, Tit. 1[:9]: A bishop "must hold firm to the sure word, so that he may be able to give instruction in sound doctrine and also to confute those who contradict it." All those things that apostles, bishops, and pastors etc. deal with by means of the word of God because those things pertain to God's kingdom and his glory and have been mandated chiefly to them, secular rulers should also deal with by means of their sword or power, to the extent possible, because both realms have been established and called to the service of God.

Christ would also have wielded the sword if God had commanded him to do so or the glory of God had required it, for, as everyone knows, he used the power that pertains to the sword when he expelled the buyers and sellers from the temple.[22] One

---

[19] Thus the anonymous memorandist; see p. 43.

[20] Cf. 1 Cor. 7:20.

[21] 2 Tim. 2:4.

[22] Mark 11:15–17.

would have to indict him as someone who had usurped the sword and confused the two realms were it not the case that both should serve the glory of God.

Moreover, when Christ relates the parable of the tares and the good seed,[23] he does not thereby forbid us to restrain false teaching, whether by means of the spiritual or the secular realm,[24] but rather will not permit us to destroy wholesome doctrine or pious Christians.

It is better to let evil men remain, if one cannot eliminate them without destroying the godly, than to destroy the godly along with them. But it does not follow from this that one should not resist those who are evil, to the extent that one can do so without harm to the godly, especially in cases where the godly cannot remain unharmed unless the evil men are separated from them.

But power is given for improvement and not for destruction;[25] therefore power must always be used to prevent the destruction of the good. God does not destroy the godly with the godless.[26] Thus he commands preachers and all his servants not to root up the wheat when they pull up the tares;[27] rather they should tolerate the wicked. But in circumstances where there is no danger to the godly, one should grant no quarter to the wicked. Thus St. Paul teaches: "Drive out the wicked person from among you."[28] In this connection Christ also says that whoever offends one of the simple Christians, it were better for him that a millstone were hanged about his neck and that he were drowned, in order to avoid such offence.[29] Therefore God also commands: "You shall not permit a sorcerer to live";[30] again, that one should execute false teachers who turn people away from God, etc.[31] Even though Christ, who came only to bring salvation,[32] does not teach or command such action, neither does he forbid it.

------

[23] Matt. 13:24–30.

[24] See the anonymous memorandum, p. 43.

[25] Cf. 2 Cor. 10:8, 13:10.

[26] Cf. Gen. 18:23, 25.

[27] See above, note 23.

[28] 1 Cor. 5:13.

[29] Matt. 18:6.

[30] Exod. 22:18, where the text actually says "sorceress."

[31] Deut. 13:1–5.

[32] Cf. Luke 19:10.

It is of no use to say[33] that this is written in the Old Testament and does not pertain to us, for the fathers in the Old Testament all "ate of the same spiritual food as we, and drank the same spiritual drink from the Rock, which is Christ.[34] That is, they had the same Spirit and faith in Christ as we have and were just as much Christians as we are. Therefore, wherein they did right, all Christians do right from the beginning of the world to the end."[35] The ten commandments too are given in the Old Testament[36] and nevertheless remain valid in the New. It is one thing to root up, destroy, or damn the tares and quite another to protect the wheat or the godly from harm, concerning which Christ speaks in this parable.[37] Therefore it does not follow from the words of Christ that he "does not want the sword of secular government in his kingdom, but rather will defend it with his word alone until the end of the world," etc.;[38] for it would necessarily follow that there were no tares in his kingdom but only pious Christians, which is contrary to the message of the parable. But since the wicked, who belong under the sword, are in Christ's kingdom but not of it, just as, similarly, believers are in the world, but not of it,[39] it follows that sword and word must go together, the sword over the wicked and the word over the good and believing. The reason that Christ did not use or establish the sword in his kingdom is that he rules and saves by his word only pious believers, who have no need of the sword for themselves; but at the same time he confirmed it and praised it as an ordinance of God over the wicked, etc.[40]

Therefore, when Isaiah says that God will fight with the breath of his mouth and smite the earth with the rod of his lips and slay the wicked,[41] he indicates the nature and the effect of the spiritual

---

[33] As had the author of the anonymous memorandum; see p. 42.

[34] 1 Cor. 10:3–4.

[35] Luther, *On Secular Authority,* AE 45:96–97.

[36] Exod. 20:2–17, Deut. 5:6–21.

[37] Matt. 13:29.

[38] Anonymous memorandum, p. 43.

[39] Cf. John 17:11, 14, 16.

[40] For example, Matt. 26:52, John 18:36. Cf. Luther, *On Secular Authority,* AE 45:93.

[41] A slightly inaccurate paraphrase of Isaiah 11:4, which the anonymous memorandist had cited; see p. 43.

kingdom of Christ and that it alone is able to overcome the devil and do all things, and without hand destroy everything that sets itself against his word, faith, and teaching.[42] For on this account he also bids his disciples to have bold confidence in him when he says: "Be of good cheer, I have overcome the world."[43]

But he does not thereby forbid that everyone, according to his calling and ability, should resist false doctrine and everything else that arises to the detriment of his kingdom, because he also commands everyone to love his neighbour[44] and prevent harm to him. One does not extinguish a fire solely with water but also with dirt, or by scattering or damping it. Thus the word and the preaching office serve most effectively against deceptive teaching; but many other means are good as well. God alone gives the growth and the fruit of his word,[45] but he nevertheless wants human beings to be his helpers and co-workers,[46] etc. Even though the Antichrist will be destroyed without hand[47] by the spirit of God alone, one can and should nevertheless always resist his evil with the hand and with all one's power.

Only the spirit of Christ can drive Satan from our hearts,[48] but we should nonetheless assist in this process by fasting, mortification of the flesh, and other exercises.[49] If we were unwilling to do this, then we would tempt God and mock his word. Censuring others also helps drive Satan out, as do mockery and other means.

That Christ did not want to be the executor of an estate,[50] that he declared to Pilate that his kingdom was not of this world,[51] and that he also forbade his disciples to exercise lordship or employ force,[52] demonstrates nothing more than that he did not want to

---

[42] Dan. 8:25; see p. 44.

[43] John 16:33.

[44] Matt. 22:39.

[45] 1 Cor. 3:6.

[46] 1 Cor. 3:9.

[47] See note 42 above.

[48] Cf. the anonymous memorandum, p. 45.

[49] Cf. Matt. 17:21 (ASV), Mark 9:29.

[50] Luke 12:14.

[51] John 18:36.

[52] Luke 22:25–26. The anonymous memorandist had cited all three of these passages; see p. 44.

make use of the secular realm, that he had not been sent for that purpose, and that he did not wish to rule by means of force and laws but rather through his spirit alone, as noted above. And although he confirmed the sword, he nevertheless did not use it, for it serves no purpose in his kingdom, to which only the godly belong. But he nonetheless defends the emperor's law and orders that taxes be paid to him,[53] thus promoting, honouring, and serving the secular realm; and he also refers the man who asked him to adjudicate his inheritance to the secular government or regular courts, because he did not want to sanction his greed and covetousness.[54] From this it follows that, in similar fashion, secular authority, where need and love do not demand it, should not intervene in the spiritual realm but should nevertheless serve and promote it.

Nor does it follow[55] that the evil seducers or false teachers should not be subject to the sword. Those who accept the word need no sword, for which reason the apostles are not supposed to exercise lordship; but all those who do not accept the word nonetheless belong under secular authority.

Now if these two realms were so completely separated that secular authority were not permitted to do or ordain anything in spiritual matters, such as teaching and ceremonies or similar things, then by the same token it would be improper for Christ, the apostles or others who belong to Christ's spiritual realm, to ordain anything concerning taxes or whatever else belongs to the secular realm. But Christ and the apostles did the opposite.[56]

In this connection one must make a distinction *inter obiectum et usum vel modum potestatis*, that is, between that which a government engages in, deals with, or is responsible for, and the method, means, or manner by which it proceeds. Christ deals with matters in the secular realm, such as marriage, taxes, and the punishment of crimes, but not in the same way that the secular realm normally does or should do. Similarly, it is proper for secular government to deal with teaching, ceremonies, and the like, all of which belong to the spiritual kingdom of Christ, but not in the

---

[53] Matt. 22:21.

[54] Luke 12:15.

[55] I.e., from the texts cited in the first sentence of the preceding paragraph.

[56] E.g., Matt. 22:21, Rom. 13:6–7.

same way that the spiritual kingdom does, that is, spiritually or offering salvation, etc. Accordingly, secular government can force no one to faith,[57] prevent no one's superstition, and master no one's conscience, for all such things should be entrusted to the word of God; but it should, nonetheless, in its own way and by its own means, promote and defend those things that serve faith, and prevent whatever hinders it, etc. For just as every individual Christian is obligated to love God with all his power and to the best of his ability,[58] and to defend and promote God's glory, so much more is a Christian who has been called to the status, office, or calling of government obligated to serve God and his kingdom, to the extent that he is able, in that capacity.

Now if one were to forbid a government to deal with anything concerning teaching or other spiritual matters, one would thereby prevent it from promoting the glory of God according to its ability. For although Christ alone in his spiritual realm instills true faith and the Holy Spirit and at the same time destroys false faith and the false spirit,[59] he nevertheless uses, as means or instruments for both purposes, men, creatures, offices, and gifts. Even though no secular government is able to do this,[60] but only Christ alone, it should nevertheless employ to this end its office no less than its own person,[61] in the service of Christ.

This does not constitute rebellious interference in Christ's office[62] but rather humble service and support of Christ according to the capacity and means of one's calling or office, etc. To interfere in Christ's realm means to usurp what belongs to him, such as the judgment of hearts, the government of consciences, and similar things, etc., or to forbid what is honourable to Christ and to command what is shameful to him; in short: to wish to be not with Christ but rather against and above Christ, etc.[63]

---

[57] As the anonymous memorandist had said; see p. 45.

[58] Cf. Matt. 22:37–38.

[59] This paraphrases the anonymous memorandum; see p. 45.

[60] I.e., instill true faith or destroy false faith.

[61] This is aimed at the anonymous memorandist; see p. 45.

[62] As claimed by the anonymous memorandist; see p. 45.

[63] Cf. Luke 11:23.

But if it is consistent with the path into Christ's kingdom for a secular government to appoint good preachers who do battle by means of the word,[64] that is, if this is useful to the spiritual kingdom, then why should a government not also dismiss or send away the evil, false, rebellious, and deceitful preachers? And if a government ought to use its authority to urge a qualified man into the preaching office, why should it not use its authority to dismiss the unqualified and banish the dangerous? And even though the government rules over no one's faith or conscience, it nevertheless does not permit public office to everyone. The kingdom of God is in the heart, as Christ says,[65] and there no government can rule; but teaching, preaching, the use of ceremonies, etc., are all external, and God's kingdom does not depend on them, even though they hinder or promote it. For that reason the government should rule over such things and administer them to the glory of God according to his command.

Let us assume also that no tumult or temporal strife were to arise as a result of false teaching,[66] and indeed that great temporal benefit, protection, and prosperity were to result from it. Nevertheless, a Christian government should, by virtue of its office, which it must use for the service of God, aggressively combat such false teaching for the sake of the glory of God, which all persons, offices, and creatures are required to uphold. The only condition is that one diligently take care that true and godly teaching not be mistaken for that which is false or iniquitous, or vice-versa. The more difficult the matter is, the more diligence and fear of God that one must bring to the task.

The princes are not at fault because they want to prevent false teaching and what is unchristian but rather because they proceed unjustly, [follow] their own opinion [rather than the truth], and execute Christ as a criminal.[67] Pilate was not censured because he executed the Galilaeans who had formed false sects,[68] nor were

---

[64] As the anonymous memorandist conceded; see p. 45.

[65] Luke 17:21.

[66] Conceding the point made by the anonymous memorandist; see p. 46.

[67] The text of this sentence is clearly incomplete and probably corrupt as well. The words in square brackets are a conjectural filling-in of the gap.

[68] This reading of Luke 13:1 may well have been influenced by the Mishna

the Jews because they defended their law,[69] but solely because, acting on the basis of misguided feelings, the fear of men, self-interest, or false understanding of the truth, they condemned the truth in Christ and the apostles, on grounds of deception, which misunderstanding St. Paul, Romans 10[:2–3], also censures in the Jews. This is to act out of ignorance of God and without faith, and to make improper use of the sword and office [of government]. This fault is found in many princes and secular governments in the present day, in that they are more fearful of temporal disorder and the reduction of their domains, or that they follow their own opinions or human doctrines more than God's word, and that they seek their own ends or temporal things rather than the glory of God or eternal things. So they heedlessly barge in, misuse their office, kill Jesus and set Barabbas free, thereby condemning their land and people as well as themselves and bringing them into danger. But if they used their sword for the protection of the truth and the punishment of error, wisely, in the fear of God, according to the word and command of the Lord, then they would be praiseworthy as servants of God.[70]

Tumult and temporal damage are not the chief reason that one should not tolerate false sects and erring rabble but, much more, the glory of God and the salvation of the soul. The sword was ordained by God for the punishment of wickedness and the reward of goodness.[71] Now wickedness is just as much the devil himself as are lies or falsehood. Therefore the government must use its sword against the devil and his kingdom in both matters. Similarly, goodness is just as much God as is truth. Therefore the government must use its sword to protect and glorify God and his kingdom. One must only take care that it not turn things around and do just the opposite.

Tumult, moreover, is not the outcome of teaching but is, rather, the product of chance or accident, for there can be both good and wicked teaching without any tumult resulting from it. Indeed,

---

Yadaim 4.8; see *The Mishna*, trans. Herbert Danby (Oxford: Clarendon Press, 1933), 785.

[69] See, for example, John 19:7, Acts 24:6 (ASV).

[70] Cf. Romans 13:4, 6.

[71] 1 Pet. 2:14.

tumult can arise without any teaching. But whether it arises or not, one must nonetheless always promote, defend, and spread the truth by means of the word and with all one's might.

One should not employ force against false teaching simply on the basis of suspicion or the fear of future danger but solely on the basis of certainty,[72] that is, after one has already established with certainty that falsehood and wickedness are found in it. And this is the opinion of Dr. Martin as well, when he writes in his letter to the princes of Saxony on the spirit of Allstedt[73] that one should combat the lying spirit with the spirit of truth, etc.,[74] that is: until by means of public truth the lying spirit is exposed, discredited and defeated, and thrown from its horse. From that point on, secular government, by virtue of its office, indeed everyone, should work toward the destruction of such a spirit. For as soon as it is publicly established that the spirit goes about with lies and false deceit, nothing is to be expected of him but murder and manslaughter etc., which everyone should prevent out of Christian love. But our princes want to execute the murderer before they ascertain the lies.

It is an uncertain, indeed an all too false supposition that someone can have false faith and not produce evil,[75] just as it is impossible to have genuine, true faith and not do good. Therefore, just as there is no evil to be awaited from true believers, so there is no good to be expected from false believers. But it is important that one not act in haste but rather inform oneself thoroughly about the matter. As soon as one is certain about the unbelief, then everyone, secular or spiritual, should work against it according to the capacity of his status or office and out of Christian devotion, not for destruction but only for improvement.[76] And then it is better that flesh and self-will should perish in order that the spirit might be saved in the day of the Lord.[77] For this is what a Christian

---

[72] As the anonymous memorandist demanded; see pp. 46–7.

[73] The work in question is Luther's *Letter to the Princes of Saxony Concerning the Rebellious Spirit* (1524). The "spirit of Allstedt" was the radical Thomas Müntzer, pastor in Allstedt, Saxony in 1523–24.

[74] See AE 40:57. The anonymous memorandist had cited this passage; see p. 49.

[75] This is aimed at the anonymous memorandist; see p. 46.

[76] Cf 2 Cor. 10:8, 13:10.

[77] Cf. 1 Cor. 5:5.

government does: punishes and kills the wicked physically so that they and others together with theirs may be preserved spiritually.

But the mobs and sects have absolutely no justification for undertaking conspiracy, tumult, or any other evil work on the ground that a government has restricted or forbidden their teaching.[78] For even if a government were so unchristian as to forbid something just, no one should commit evil on that account. For example: one finds governments that forbid the administration of the sacrament in both forms, which is patently unjust and contrary to Christ. If you do not wish to participate under one form but rather, according to Christ's command, under both forms, you must not on that account resist the government, act contrary to Christian love, or wantonly instigate some evil, but rather move to some other place where you are free to observe the sacrament according to Christ's institution. For even though the government is wrong to forbid this to you and should not lord it over your faith, the city is nevertheless under its authority and it can, moreover, forbid the city to you, and rather than act against the government, it is your duty to leave its territory, region, or city.

The reason that the apostles and other pious Christians preached against the will and without the knowledge of the government[79] is that they were driven by the Holy Spirit to fulfil the command of God, who is the lord of all lands; it is improper for anyone to oppose his word and truth. Thus also the children of Israel justly robbed the Egyptians, annihilated the heathen, etc., because he ordered them to do so.[80] But everyone is of necessity obligated to combat Satan and his lies. To the extent that each government is bound by God's command to love God with all its heart, all its soul, and all its might, and its neighbour as itself,[81] it is equally obligated to use its office to the glory of God and to prevent whatever brings him dishonour.

The advice of Gamaliel, Acts 5[:38–39], does not contradict this.[82] For Gamaliel knew that the teaching of the apostles was true; thus

---

[78] This is aimed at the anonymous memorandist; see p. 47.

[79] Cf. the anonymous memorandum, p. 46.

[80] See Exod. 12:35–36; Deut. 20:16–18; Josh. 6:17, 24, 8:2, 26, 10:28–40, 11:10–12.

[81] Luke 10:27–28.

[82] Contra the anonymous memorandist; see p. 48.

he sought to prevent the Jews from persecuting it and acting contrary to their own consciences, for they themselves had been so struck by the miracles and the godly conduct of the apostles that they were taken aback and could not with certainty condemn their teaching as false.[83] For this reason the Jews had to choose the safest, least dangerous course in an uncertain matter. That is what Gamaliel recommended. But if it had been a case of a doctrine that had been proved [false] beyond any reasonable doubt, the pious Gamaliel would have recommended that it be extirpated, in strict accordance with the law of God in Deuteronomy 13[:1–5].

In our own day we advise all governments to take no action against anyone for reasons of doctrine unless they are absolutely sure that the doctrine is false and deceitful; otherwise they should not interfere. Therefore, let them take care not to allow themselves to be persuaded by priests and bishops to butt in frivolously, without well-grounded judgment, for they are not supposed to render judgment in any matter without a hearing and adequate investigation.

But this does not mean that a Christian, God-fearing government should follow the example of Gallio,[84] who, as a godless man, did not want to concern himself with divine matters, and out of sloth reject the burden of such important matters that touch the glory of God and the salvation of souls. For it would thereby reject God, like unfaithful servants who had not wished to devote themselves to his affairs and only did what contributed to their own glory.

Nor can a government in good conscience deal with matters pertaining to doctrine by avoiding them and referring them to Moses and the prophets.[85] For it is the duty of a government to know the law of God, to follow it, and to conduct its office according to it. For this reason God has commanded that a king, when he takes the throne, shall take the law of God from the priests and Levites and have a copy of it written in a book that shall remain with him, and that he shall read in it all his life, so that he may learn to fear the Lord, his God, and keep all the words of this law and do them.[86] But

---

[83] Cf. Acts 4:13–16.

[84] Acts 18:12–16. Contra the anonymous memorandist; see p. 48.

[85] The anonymous memorandist had cited Luke 16:29, 31; see p. 48.

[86] Deut. 17:18–19.

if our governments wish to deal with cases involving doctrine or similar matters according to imperial or papal law and undertake executions or other rash actions, let them see to it that they proceed fairly.

Paul's statement that there must be sects in order that the elect may be recognized, etc.,[87] does not mean that one must therefore not take defensive measures against them.[88] For Christ, our dear Lord, himself says: "Offences must come."[89] Nevertheless, all Christians, each according to his status and ability, should endeavour to prevent all such offences. For just as it is the nature of Satan and his servants to sow offences, so it is the practice of Christ and his servants to gather them up and throw them away.[90] There must be sects because Satan exists. But we must not respond with silence, and the government must not cease to act against them. For the true servants and stewards of God are recognized when they, wide awake and diligent, offer resistance.[91] When, by contrast, the unfaithful, lazy servants sleep and are not watchful, the enemy comes and sows tares among the wheat.[92]

Even if Satan does rage and the false sects do grow and become defiant when one takes action against them,[93] one must not on that account refrain from such action. For God inflicts this as a test of the faithful, so that their faith might be the more sharply challenged when they see such great constancy among the sectarians and that afterwards they might appear all the more glorious when they do not allow themselves to be led from the way of truth. Equally, God may well impose this defiant constancy of the fanatics in order to shame the godless, so that they might become the more doubtful and inconstant in spirit and, like those who are delirious, not know which way is which, because Satan himself bears witness against their inconstancy. Thus we see that a government that takes action against the false, erroneous teaching of the sects, but does so out

---

[87] 1 Cor. 11:19.

[88] Rejecting the conclusion of the anonymous memorandist; see p. 49.

[89] Matt. 18:7.

[90] Matt. 13:39, 41.

[91] Cf. Luke 12:37, 42.

[92] Matt. 13:25.

[93] Thus the anonymous memorandist; see pp. 49–50.

of pure tyranny, without the fear or the word of God, on the basis of personal opinion or human laws, will in the end become just as desperate, frightened, and confused in its conscience as was the pharaoh over the plagues in Egypt.[94] This is not because the secular government acts according to the means of its office against false doctrines but rather because the godless tyrants abuse their office unjustly *et, quod justum est, non iuste exequuntur*,[95] and thus become fools. Therefore, it is still true that because a government is not blameworthy when it uses its sword against the deceivers in an appropriate way, the devil will not really make its sword dull.[96] Let the government only see to it that it not use the sword frivolously, for the sake of its own glory, but rather solely in the fear of God and in the service of his glory. Even if the result is only an immediate increase in the number of unbelievers, the blame cannot be laid upon the government. For frequently the same thing happens when one employs the word against deceitful teaching, namely that the number of unbelievers only goes up. It is not that the word or even the sword are at fault but that Satan and his hordes lie concealed like hornets in a hollow tree so that no one realizes that there are so many of them.[97] But if one disturbs them, the size of the whole swarm becomes apparent. Thus Satan vaingloriously inaugurates his kingdom with a great horde, hoping to overwhelm by surprise those who struggle against him, and he succeeds in rendering fainthearted those who have not begun this struggle by word and sword with God.

Nor can one refrain from using force in a Christian manner against deceitful doctrines on the ground that this example would justify godless governments in taking action against true believers,[98] although the argument that the government should not impose the death penalty for reasons of doctrine is to be taken

---

[94] Exod. 12:30–32.

[95] I.e., "and, that which is just is not carried out justly." Cf. the similarly worded passage in Pseudo-Dionysius Areopagita, Ep. 8:1: "...quae justa sunt, non secundum dignitatem exsequi"; J.P. Migne, ed., *Patrologiae cursus completus...series graeca* (Paris: Apud Garnier Fratres Editores, et J.–P. Migne, Successores, 1857–1912) 3:1091A.

[96] As claimed by the anonymous memorandist; see p. 50.

[97] Job 10 is cited in the margin, but Ps. 10:9 seems the more likely reference.

[98] Contra the anonymous memorandum; see pp. 50–1.

seriously. For when I asked the advice of Dr. Martin on this question, he replied in writing as follows: "You ask whether it is appropriate for a government to put false teachers to death. Answer: I hesitate to approve the death penalty even where there are sufficient legal grounds. In this matter I am anxious lest anyone follow the example provided by the papists and by the Jews at the time of Christ, among whom, since their law decreed that false, deceitful teachers and heretics were to be put to death, it eventually reached the point that no one but holy prophets and innocent people were executed by virtue of this law, so that godless governments followed their example and made false teachers or heretics out of whomever and however many as they pleased. I fear that the same thing will happen with our governments if it were to be established with one example that it is proper to put false teachers to death, because at the present time we still see that among the papists the misuse of this law results in innocent blood being shed for guilty. For this reason I can by no means sanction the execution of false teachers. It is enough that they be expelled. Even if our successors were to misuse this penalty, they would still sin less and only harm themselves."[99] Thus Luther. It follows that it is appropriate for government to impose punishments on the deceivers, but cautiously, not out of tyranny, etc.

As for the Bohemians, they have employed the sword a great deal in matters pertaining to doctrine.[100] But if they and perhaps other governments as well achieved little thereby and even had more disorder than other governments who remained quiet, we will commend that to God's judgment, for we are speaking here *de jure* and not *de facto*. Perhaps these governments did not act with good reason or with appropriate moderation, just as people frequently undertake something under the appearance and title of

---

[99] The text is the author's own German translation of Luther's Latin letter to Linck of 14 July 1528. See WA–Br 4:498–99, where, however, the passage cited here is not properly integrated into the text of the letter, an error noted and corrected in ibid., 14:XXII–XXV. On the problem that this citation creates for determining the authorship of this memorandum, see the introduction, pp. 17–18.

[100] An apparent reference to the Hussite wars, 1420–34. This is aimed at the anonymous memorandist; see p. 51.

the gospel but with great villainy concealed underneath. May God turn it all to the best. Amen.

This is what I wanted to say, hastily and on the spur of the moment, in reply to the arguments that may prompt others as well to demonstrate that such arguments support nothing more than a finding of the abuse of power.[101] But it remains true that a government has the Christian duty to take action in matters affecting doctrine and worship, that it may do so with a good conscience, and that it must not remain silent and tolerate all manner of false sects.

Should the government of a city permit every sect to preach, organize, appoint and dismiss teachers, just as it pleases and without objection,[102] then the regular government would in that case be unnecessary. Indeed, there would be as many governments as there are sects. The lawful government would have to abandon its office and give way to the sects. What then would remain of God's ordinance or of Paul's command that everything should be done "decently and in order"?[103] Also: "Let everyone be subject to the governing authorities."[104] The sects would, in this matter at least, be free from obedience to government and the popish exemption of the clerical factions[105] would be powerfully confirmed. But if this papal exemption, even though it be sanctioned by the emperor, is unchristian and against God's word and ordinance,[106] as no jurist doubts, how much more would this concession destroy all divine and human order. It would have to follow that any government that refused to tolerate any guild or brotherhood of artisans (which is a much less serious matter than factious sects of teachers etc.) acted unjustly.[107]

---

[101]I.e., the most that the anonymous memorandist can demonstrate is that some governments have abused their legitimate power in matters of religion.

[102]As demanded by the anonymous memorandist in his letter to Lazarus Spengler; see p. 52.

[103]1 Cor. 14:40.

[104]Rom. 13:1.

[105]"Die gaistlichen secten," i.e., the Catholic clergy, especially the religious orders.

[106]I.e., Rom. 13:1–7, 1 Pet. 2:13–17.

[107]In this period, the government of Nürnberg did not allow independent guilds but kept the regulation of the economic life of the city in its own hands.

But if one were to allow each sect freely to preach those doctrines and observe those ceremonies by which they hope to come to God,[108] why does holy scripture forbid that anyone should follow his own opinions or the feelings of his heart?[109] What would be the need of any government or the regulations of divine law, according to which we must live and behave? By this method parents would not be allowed to take the stick to their children and the government could punish no one. For if a government should or must silently endure the erroneous teachings of its subjects, how much more must it do so in the case of many other evil desires or moral offences, which are by no means as serious as deceitful teaching, because the latter distorts and poisons the very basis of human conduct and because all vices have their root and origin in erroneous delusions. If one should not resist the origin or the root, so much less should one resist the fruits that grow from it. That would be to scratch the surface and to ignore what is underneath, to cut off the branch and to leave the trunk and the roots untouched, so that finally the last state must be worse than the first.[110] I will say nothing of many ordinances,[111] which every sensible man can judge for himself.

---

[108] Allusion to the anonymous memorandist's letter to Spengler; see p. 52.

[109] Cf. Num. 15:39, Isa. 65:2.

[110] Cf. Matt. 12:45, Luke 11:26.

[111] I.e., human ordinances, in contrast to the "regulations of divine law" mentioned in the second sentence of the paragraph.

Document Number Five

Whether Secular Christian Government Has the
Power to Ban False Preachers or Erring Sects and to
Establish Order in Ecclesiastical Affairs
[Wenzeslaus Linck or Andreas Osiander,
before 26 March 1530]

It is indeed a difficult and worrisome matter to determine exactly
how far the power of secular government extends, for horrible and
unbearable harm results if it is given too much room, while it is
also not without harm if it is too narrowly confined. Nevertheless,
it is better that it should be confined and punish too little than that
it should go too far and punish too much. For it is always better
to let a rogue live than to kill a good man, since the world is full
of rogues and always will be, while good men are scarce.[1]

But one must always zealously take care that the door not be
opened to the wantonness of godless, dangerous, deceptive people, who harm simple people with their lies, when they[2] claim that
they are "spiritual," exempt from all government etc., whereby they
seek to do evil without retribution; or when they falsely maintain
that the secular government does not have the power to summon
a council or by suitable means to establish order in spiritual matters
in order that godless abuses might be abolished and that whatever
serves the glory of God and the common weal might be undertaken
and promoted.

---

[1] This paragraph is a very close paraphrase of the passage from Luther's *On
Secular Authority* found in AE 45:104–5.

[2] I.e., the godless people. Here the reference is to the Catholic hierarchy.

Further, one must carefully note those things concerning which secular government has the power to judge, order, and command. As St. Peter so splendidly puts it, when he says: "Submit yourselves to every ordinance of man for the Lord's sake."[3] Now no human ordinance can possibly extend as far as heaven, over God, angels, souls, consciences, or anything on earth that no one can either see or hear, but solely to earth over the external dealings of men with one another which men can see, know, judge, condemn, or absolve.[4] Beyond that, no one owes them obedience, as St. Paul declares that one should render to them honour, custom, tribute, fear, and that which is earthly.[5] Our Lord Jesus Christ proclaims the same thing when he says: "Render unto Caesar the things which are Caesar's, and unto God the things that are God's."[6] Whatever is on earth and belongs to the temporal, earthly kingdom, over that the government has power from God. But whatever is divine and belongs to the eternal kingdom, that is in the power of the heavenly lord alone,[7] as David says in the psalm:[8] "The heavens are the Lord's, but the earth he gave to the children of men" when at the creation he gave them dominion over animals, birds, fish, and all that is on the earth.[9] Thus also St. Peter sets limits to human authority when he says: "We ought to obey God rather than men."[10] Moreover, one must here diligently consider that in all things, but chiefly those having to do with faith, doctrine, souls, or God, one should act not merely with force, by virtue of secular authority alone, but far more in the spirit of Christian service, with love and always in the fear of God. For the secular realm was not established for its own sake, but rather that it might serve the kingdom of God and increase and promote that kingdom as much as possible, as we sing in the song and as Christ has commanded: "What I have done and what I've said / shall be thy doing, teaching / so that God's kingdom may be spread / all

---

[3] 1 Pet. 2:13.

[4] Cf. Luther, *On Secular Government,* AE 45:111.

[5] Rom. 13:7.

[6] Matt. 22:21.

[7] See above, note 4.

[8] Ps. 115:16.

[9] Gen. 1:28.

[10] Acts 5:29.

to his glory reaching."[11] Wherefore St. Paul also says that government is God's servant for the reward of those that do good and for the punishment of those that do evil.[12] Therefore, we are speaking here not simply of government as such according to its power, but rather of Christian government, that is, a government that would gladly use its power in a Christian fashion for the glory of god and the service of man, and which in its office does not seek its own advantage or profit but rather, as St. Paul teaches, only "the profit of many, that they may be saved."[13] Wherefore it is not our intention mightily to exalt secular authority and thus sanction the arrogance of its godless, haughty tyranny, but only to show God-fearing rulers how to make proper use of their power.

Hence the following proposition:

Although those things that pertain immediately and of necessity to the spiritual realm should be dealt with in a spiritual manner and be entrusted to the clergy, who have the office of the word; nevertheless, to the extent that such things are external or earthly and can be separated from the spiritual realm, a Christian magistrate may and should deal with them, unhindered, for the protection and promotion of the truth.

This proposition has two parts, each of which contains several points, for which reason we want to explain them.

First, the proposition speaks of those things that belong of necessity to the kingdom of God or to the spiritual government of the conscience etc., for the sake of external, transitory ceremonies, which contribute nothing to salvation. God has not commanded such ceremonies but rather men have established them because of their own devotion or for other reasons; they are human ordinances and thus belong under that authority that is not under discussion at the moment, and they are not very important anyway. For

---

[11] This is from the last verse of Luther's hymn, "Dear Christians, Let Us Now Rejoice" (1523), AE 53:220. The words that Luther puts into Jesus' mouth are probably a conflation of several biblical texts, including Matt. 28:20, John 13:15, and perhaps Matt. 6:10. Thanks are due to Gottfried Seebaß for supplying this information.

[12] Rom. 13:3–4.

[13] 1 Cor. 10:33.

example: ecclesiastical goods, taxes, income, privileges, jewels, buildings, vestments, and the like. No one can deny that these are worldly, temporal things, pertaining to the secular realm. It is beyond dispute that the secular government should order and administer such things according to justice and the needs of the case, regardless of the exceptions or immunities that the clergy have devised for themselves according to papal laws, contrary to all Christian love and fraternity, without God's word and even contrary to it, which word teaches that we should bear one another's burdens and so fulfil the law of Christ.[14] For Christ left the one commandment that we should love and serve one another.[15] The members of the so-called spiritual estate exclude themselves from this by their privileges and exemptions, misusing these solely as a cover for sin and devious wantonness. They extend their exemption to all their pleasures, insisting that even their whores, dogs, and fools are spiritual and thus exempt from secular authority. Against this St. Paul says: "For, brethren, you have been called to liberty; only use not liberty for an occasion to the flesh, but by love serve one another."[16]

Public preaching, the orderly administration of the sacraments, which Christ himself commanded and established as part of his kingdom, and whatever similar works or practices might exist, which are necessary and useful for faith, love, repose of the conscience, or the pastoral office: all these things follow from the spiritual government of souls or the kingdom of God and are a necessary result of it. Concerning them one may dispute whether they belong to the secular realm or solely to the spiritual realm.

Second, it was said that such things should be entrusted to the clergy, who are the regularly designated ministers for that purpose, from whose mouth one should seek God's will and law,[17] in order that all be done decently and in order[18] and without confusion, as would happen[19] if one member of the body were to usurp the office

---

[14] Gal. 6:2.

[15] John 13:34, 15:12, 17.

[16] Gal. 5:13.

[17] Mal. 2:7.

[18] 1 Cor. 14:40.

[19] The balance of this paragraph is a paraphrase of the passage from Luther's

of another. Thus the devil plays tricks on us and stages a comedy in that the bishops ignore God's word and their spiritual office, pay no heed to souls, but rather concern themselves with secular government. On the other hand, the secular rulers do not use their sword against evil works like murder, adultery, blasphemy, usury, robbery, etc., things they are stuck in up to their ears, but rather against doctrine, faith, or heresies. Thus they do things backwards, wishing to rule souls with the sword and the body with interdicts and words, making princes of bishops and vice-versa, until the devil leads princes and bishops to hell.

There is in all Christians one spirit, but many diverse gifts.[20] They all have one lord but diverse offices. Therefore, no one should interfere in another's office, not even by citing the authority or the name of God, for God is not a God of confusion but of peace.[21] "No soldier on service gets entangled in civilian pursuits."[22] In exactly the same way, no bishop or minister of the word should interfere in the business of secular government. And again, Christ refused to be a judge or executor of temporal goods[23] because he had not come to establish a secular realm but a divine one. Similarly, the apostles adhered to their vocation and preaching office so strictly that they did not wish to be burdened with the care of the poor, which nevertheless appertains to bishops, because this might interfere with their preaching office. As they said: "It is not right that we should leave the word of God and serve tables."[24] Therefore, let everyone remain in the vocation to which God has called him: let the shepherd of souls exercise the spiritual rule over consciences, and let the secular government exercise its power over secular affairs.

Third, the proposition asserts that nevertheless a Christian magistrate etc., who also cares for the kingdom of God, to which he belongs and into which he hopes to come, for which reason he

---

On Secular Authority found in AE 45:115–16.

[20] 1 Cor. 12:4ff.

[21] 1 Cor. 14:33.

[22] 2 Tim. 2:4.

[23] Luke 12:14. The anonymous memorandist had cited this passage in support of his own argument; see p. 44.

[24] Acts 6:2.

desires not merely to rule and be served as a lord but also to serve others in Christian love as a Christian in his office of government, to the glory of God:[25] it is appropriate that such a ruler also use his office for the promotion and protection of the kingdom of God in spiritual matters. "To the pure," faithful man "all things are pure."[26] Such a man has power over all things, but he is careful to use all things for welfare and improvement.[27] "But to the corrupt and unbelieving nothing is pure." They cannot even use their own office properly, much less help others, "for their minds and consciences are both corrupted,"[28] so that they are defiled and spotted with sin in all that they undertake. They seek only themselves and what is theirs in all things and not the glory of God or the well-being of their neighbour. Therefore, when they exercise government, they lord it over people, arrogantly flaunting their power, as tyrants do, so that it does them no good to meddle in spiritual matters, because their own secular rule brings them damnation. But those that are Christian have the spirit of Christ which makes them spiritual, and they can judge all things without danger or disadvantage to anyone. For in their rule they do not seek themselves or what is theirs[29] but only how they may promote the glory of God and the welfare of all, for which reason they act humbly and in the fear of God, safely, unable to do harm. We have a beautiful example of this in Saul, whom God made king, and when he was anointed, Samuel said: "Do whatever your hand finds to do; for God is with you."[30]

Fourth, the proposition says: to the extent that things are external etc.; for according to this criterion they belong under secular government. In this connection it is to be noted that there is no one on earth so spiritual that he is not at the same time carnal and thus under the sword. Thus St. Paul subjects all men, no matter how holy or spiritual, when he says: "Let everyone be subject to

---

[25] Here the author abandons the sentence structure inaugurated by the "that" in the first line.

[26] Titus 1:15.

[27] Cf. 1 Cor. 2:15, 10:23–4.

[28] Titus 1:15.

[29] Cf. 1 Cor. 6:2, 10:33.

[30] 1 Sam. 10:7.

the governing authorities."[31] Since all men are subject to government, so must everything that a man has or does be subject to it, in so far as it is external and known to the government.

Now we wish to amplify and prove our proposition.

Demonstration of the First Part

First, Paul says that spiritual matters must be judged spiritually, for no one knows what is godly or in God without the spirit of God.[32] The natural man, however, who is without grace, does not receive the spirit of God; it is foolishness to him, he cannot know it, for it must be perceived spiritually. The wisdom of the gospel is not like the wisdom of this world, which comes to nought; none of the princes of this world have known it, etc. Moreover, in spiritual matters "we wrestle not against flesh and blood, but against principalities, against powers, against the rulers of the darkness of this world, against spiritual wickedness in high places."[33] For this one needs the armour of God;[34] no worldly sword is of any help. One must never struggle in a carnal manner, for the weapons of Christian knighthood "are not carnal, but mighty through God, to the pulling down of strongholds; casting down imaginings and every high thing that exalts itself against the knowledge of God, and bringing into captivity every thought to the obedience of Christ; and having in a readiness to revenge all disobedience."[35]

These words clearly show that secular, human power is capable of doing nothing in spiritual matters, for it cannot know them. What kind of a judicial process would it be if one wished to exercise power over things which can be neither seen, heard, nor known? The church itself does not judge secret, unknown things but only public things. How then should secular power judge spiritual matters, such as faith or unbelief, which belong to the kingdom of God?[36] "Heresy is a spiritual thing which you cannot hack to pieces

---

[31] Rom. 13:1.

[32] 1 Cor. 2:10–14.

[33] Eph. 6:12.

[34] Eph. 6:11, 13.

[35] 2 Cor. 10:4–6. Cf. Luther, *On Secular Authority,* AE 45:114.

[36] Cf. ibid., 107.

with iron, consume with fire,"[37] or destroy with any secular power. Divine power and the spiritual armour of the word must combat it. If that does not work, secular power will also be ineffective if, like unreasoning beasts, it interferes by means of the sword without God's word. Through the error of heresies the devil possesses men's hearts. Therefore, one must lighten the darkness of such erring hearts by means of the word and not kill by fire, water, sword, or power the vessel in which the devil lies concealed. The devil fears no power on earth; he regards iron as straw and does not flee the sword from which even the mighty of this world flee.[38] Thus one must defend and uphold the spiritual kingdom of God, not with secular power but with divine power, that is, with the word of the gospel of Christ, which is a power of God that saves all who believe it.[39] God's kingdom does not come with external gestures, for it is inward in the heart.[40] It is not eating, drinking or external deeds, "but righteousness, peace, and joy in the Holy Ghost."[41] But just as the kingdom of God and the service of God exist only in spirit and in truth[42] and not in external acts, for which reason it must be ruled with the divine power of the spirit and the sceptre of God's word,[43] so also must it be with everything that pertains and is necessary to it, even though it be external and temporal. But this then raises a question concerning preaching or public teaching: since this is an external thing bound to time, place, and person (over which the secular government unquestionably has power) while yet pertaining to the spiritual kingdom of God, to whom should one assign its administration? The same question applies to other spiritual matters.

Demonstration of the Second Part

FIRST.[44] Although the spiritual and secular realms are distinct and have different offices, they are nevertheless not opposed to one

---

[37] Quotation from ibid., 114.

[38] Job 41:26–28. Cf. Luther, op. cit., 115.

[39] Rom. 1:16.

[40] Luke 17:20–21.

[41] Rom. 14:17.

[42] Cf. John 4:23–24.

[43] A point that the anonymous memorandist had made; see pp. 42–3.

[44] The "demonstration" is divided into two sections. This first section, which

another, so that one may not exist alongside the other, or that a person who has office in one may not participate in the administration of the other, in the way that Christ's kingdom and Satan's kingdom are opposed, so that he who is not with Christ is against him, and whoever does not gather with him scatters;[45] no one can serve both God and mammon;[46] Christ has no concord with Belial, righteousness no fellowship with unrighteousness, and the light no communion with darkness.[47] On the contrary, it is the same as with law and gospel, which are both God's word, given for man's salvation, even though each works differently upon the conscience. For the law kills, but the gospel awakens and gives life,[48] and this is because of our imperfection, for we have become so deformed through the old Adam that Christ cannot rise in us unless the old Adam die first.[49] God cannot save us unless he damn us, as Isaiah [28:21] says that the Lord will rise up and be wroth, that he may do his work, which is nevertheless not his work, and perform his deed, which is nevertheless not his deed. [In other words,] our nature is so evil that God cannot be gracious to us (which is his proper work) unless he first work harm or evil upon us by harsh measures (which is not his proper work). For as the world does not know God through wisdom, so he must bring his own to himself through folly, cross, and suffering.[50] If he did not crucify the flesh, the spirit would not live in us. Thus also the spiritual and secular realms are ordinances of God, established for the good of man, in order that the body and all that belongs to the body might be ruled by the secular realm, and the soul or conscience and all that pertains to the soul by the spiritual realm.

Now it is a fact that soul and body are so united that they do not willingly part from one another. What affects the soul also affects the body and vice-versa, so that usually neither experiences suffering or comfort, good or evil, gain or loss, apart from the other.

---

is by far the longer, runs to page 110.

[45] Luke 11:23.

[46] Matt 6:24, Luke 16:13.

[47] 2 Cor. 6:14–15.

[48] Cf. 2 Cor. 3:6.

[49] Cf. Rom. 6:3–13.

[50] 1 Cor. 1:17ff.

If the body is sick, one cannot properly help it back to health unless one also helps the soul. Similarly, confidence in the physician or other mental attitudes have a great effect upon a sick person. One should think of spiritual and secular government in exactly the same way, namely that one cannot fruitfully exercise spiritual government by the word if the secular government does not cooperate. Thus St. Paul exhorts us to pray first of all for secular government, "that we may lead a quiet and peaceable life in all godliness and honesty," so that other men too will "come to the knowledge of the truth," which is pleasing to God.[51] We see from these words of St. Paul that no one can live honourably or in a Christian manner or effectively preach the gospel if the secular government does not function properly as well. Therefore, God wills that everyone be subject to secular government and helpful to it, so that governments will not have cause to hinder the gospel or God's kingdom, but will rather be moved to support it. And, on the one hand, just as Christ paid the tax that he did not owe, simply in order not to offend the officials,[52] so even more, on the other hand, secular government can never profitably be exercised or endure if spiritual government does not function properly. Thus both are so completely bound together and involved with one another that each with its office should be of use to the other.

It follows from this that, just as spiritual government, by means of preaching the word and its other offices, strives to produce not only consciences that have spotless faith in God and untainted love[53] toward their neighbour but also impeccable behaviour in all civil, human dealings and whatever pertains to the secular realm, that is, to render obedience and to pay taxes to the government and to give everyone his due—as Christ, the supreme king in the spiritual realm illustrates by words and examples, when he teaches that taxes should be paid to the emperor,[54] himself pays duty[55] and whatever else is due the government, and so forth, although he does not venture to wield the sword or exercise secular govern-

---

[51] 1 Tim. 2:1–4.

[52] Matt. 17:24–27.

[53] Cf. 2 Cor. 6:6, 1 Tim. 1:5.

[54] Matt. 22:15–21.

[55] Matt. 17:24–27.

ment, for he is not sent or called by God for that purpose, but uses the spiritual sceptre, which he holds in God's kingdom, and his preaching office for the help, assistance, maintenance, and service of the secular realm; after him, the beloved apostles and all pious Christians have done and taught the same, as we read in the histories that through their intercession, wholesome doctrine, and Christian practices, whole lands and cities have been maintained in good secular order and prosperity,—in exactly the same way[56] the secular government should use its office or sword for the service and promotion of the divine, spiritual realm, for it is on this account that government is called "the minister of God."[57] And even though it is true that God alone could maintain his kingdom by his almighty power, without the help of any creature, nevertheless he wishes to use the secular kingdom for this purpose, in order thereby to make his goodness all the more evident and to inculcate and test the exercise of love and faithfulness among men. God could also grant his spirit without external preaching, sacraments, and everything else that pertains to the spiritual, evangelical kingdom of God, and do everything through himself alone. But his great wisdom and goodness would not be so evident to angels and men. Neither would they have as much cause or opportunity to love and serve one another to the glory and pleasure of God. Thus St. Paul says: "We are labourers together with God: you are God's husbandry, God's building."[58] He gives and does all directly through men, whom he takes as his helpers, in order that through such help and external preaching the manifold wisdom of God be made known to the principalities and powers in the heavenly places.[59] For "although the angels in heaven are full of God" and gaze upon his face, wherein they can perceive his will and pleasure, "they nevertheless experience daily the new graces and gifts that God bestows on Christendom,"[60] from which they recog-

---

[56] By now the author has lost control of his boa constrictor of a sentence. The remaining phrase is dependent upon the "that" in the first line of the paragraph.

[57] Rom. 13:4.

[58] 1 Cor. 3:9.

[59] Eph. 3:8–10.

[60] Quotation from Luther's marginal gloss on the key-word "furstenthumen" (principalities) in Eph. 3:10; WA–DB 7:198.

nize more and more his wisdom, goodness, and righteousness, though they can never search out its depths. Thus they always experience a special new joy in God's works as often as he converts a sinner to repentance and receives him with grace.[61] Should they then not also rejoice if God manifests to many others secular or eternal salvation and comfort through a man in secular or spiritual government? The angels of the lands struggle with one another in that each seeks the welfare of its own land,[62] for which reason they recognize and praise the goodness of God when a pious prince rules his land peacefully in the fear of God, as Joseph provided for Egypt in time of famine.[63] From this we can understand that where those in the spiritual realm do not serve the secular realm and vice-versa, the glory of God is diminished and brotherly love hindered, for the sake of which, however, both kingdoms were established by God. It is just as though one hand were not to clean the other or help in its work. One must not be concerned about which needs the other, nor imagine that the spiritual kingdom has no need of the secular. Instead, one must think only of the mildness and goodness of God, who wishes to be honoured in both kingdoms when they support one another in brotherly love.

This cannot be labelled tumult, much less wanton interference in God's kingdom,[64] since each kingdom remains in the office entrusted to it and uses it faithfully for the benefit of the other.[65] The preachers teach and exercise spiritual government not merely for the comfort of consciences, the strengthening of faith or increase of the spirit, but also for the censure of public vices, the maintenance of external peace, and similar things that belong to the secular realm. On the other hand, the secular rulers wield the sword and use their power not merely to achieve temporal peace, civic sustenance, the censure of vice, and the reward of virtue[66] but also for the protection of Christian teaching, the implanting of

---

[61] Luke 15:10.

[62] The reference is to Daniel's vision of conflict in heaven among the angelic patrons of the nations; see Dan. 10, esp. verses 13, 20.

[63] Gen. 41:43–57.

[64] As claimed by the anonymous memorandist; see p. 45.

[65] A particularly awkward paragraph break has been eliminated here.

[66] Cf. 1 Pet. 2:14.

faith, and the repression of rebels, in order that the faithful might live peacefully in godliness[67] and that simple consciences might not be disturbed by godless seducers. It would be a tumultuous, diabolical confusion if one abandoned its calling, refused to use its own office, and interfered in the office of the other, as, for example, if the government were to forget the sword and wished to usurp the office of pastor or preacher, which has not been entrusted to it; or, on the other hand, if a bishop were to abandon preaching and take up the sword without a command. This would be a disorderly confounding of the regimes. But when a prince stands by the pastor with his power and helps to repress, rescue, or promote that which pertains to the kingdom of God, to the extent that he can with his power; or when the pastor, on the other hand, stands by the prince with praying, preaching, admonition, etc., then each remains in his calling, Moses stands by Aaron, and each gets his due.

Samuel was a prophet of the Lord and a judge over the people, had both offices, served the divine and the secular kingdoms— quite properly, for God had entrusted him with both.[68] The same was true of Abraham and many other holy fathers. And why should not God be pleased to entrust both to one man? Every Christian is both priest and king, as St. Peter says: "You are a chosen race, a royal priesthood" etc.[69] If God entrusts both to one person, he also gives him the strength to exercise both without harm. But if anyone were disobedient and neglected both, or if only one office were entrusted to him and he, neglecting it, assumed the other, which had not been entrusted to him, he would be an unfaithful rogue.

But the reason that Christ and the apostles and other holy teachers did not want to assume secular government[70] is not that both kingdoms cannot stand together but rather that God had only entrusted them with spiritual government. Nor was it because they had condemned or rejected secular government, as though no apostle or pious Christian could exercise it, but only in order that they might not thereby be distracted from the kingdom of God.

---

[67] Cf. 1 Tim. 2:2.

[68] See 1 Sam. 3:19–21, 7:6, 15–17; Acts 13:20.

[69] 1 Pet. 2:9.

[70] An argument advanced by the anonymous memorandist; see p. 44.

Which happens if one places one's trust in secular government or seeks wealth through it.

And in order that we might understand this better, let us look at the words of Christ where he says: "The secular kings exercise lordship and the mighty are called gracious lords; but you shall not be so."[71] With this saying he does not forbid or condemn secular government as something unchristian or that a Christian or an apostle may not exercise. Rather, he only shows the proper use of power and forbids heathen misuse. For among the heathen it happens that those who wish to be called lords and who out of ambition seek high honours oppress and despise other people, as at first Nimrod began to be a mighty man on earth and was a mighty hunter before the lord,[72] that is, he ruled by force, ripping and devouring like a wild boar or bear, oppressing other people, always seeking nothing more than to conquer and subject as many lands as possible, all of which is the way of heathen rulers, who exercise lordship and proceed with force. Christ condemns this and forbids his apostles and all Christians to do it. But the sword and temporal government he does not forbid, nor does he abolish it. This is completely obvious from the text. For when the apostles began to be indignant at the two sons of Zebedee because they strove after government and quarrelled with one another over precedence,[73] which was sinful, offensive, and arrogant, the Lord reproved them for it and showed them that it was heathen, unchristian, and antisocial. For the heathen, who do not place their trust in God alone, seek great things or honour before the world, rely more on the power of their lordship than on God's help, and do not use their power for the service or love of their neighbour but only for their own luxury and wantonness. None of this becomes a Christian or pious person, who only wishes to be of use to everyone in common and takes no thought for himself. This is not what a pious lord should do, who gives his life for his subjects, as Christ himself did.[74] Thus Christ does not say that there

---

[71] Luke 22:25–26; cf. Mark 10:42–43. The anonymous memorandist had cited this as one of his proof texts; see p. 44.

[72] Gen. 10:8–9.

[73] Mark 10:35ff.; Luke 22:24.

[74] Mark 10:45.

should be no orderly government among Christians, but only that it should not be conducted as the heathens do it. Christian government serves faith and love, the heathen do not do this, etc.

Similarly, we read that when the children of Israel demanded a king,[75] God hesitated,[76] not because orderly government displeased him, for previously he had always given them judges and lords and had also, through Moses, given laws about whom they should chose as king and how he should conduct himself in office,[77] but rather God was displeased because they placed their trust in the king after the manner of the heathen, as though he would protect them from their enemies, and thus they abandoned God. For this reason, the lord proclaimed that because they were behaving like heathen, their king would treat them in a heathen, tyrannical manner.[78] Government is divine, beneficial, and good, but tyranny is evil and harmful, the rod of divine wrath,[79] for he gives hypocrites as overlords,[80] who oppress and torment the people with onerous taxes and tyrannical laws; he makes boys princes and allows infantile rule[81] when he wants to vent his wrath.[82]

But that Christ, by means of the saying "You shall not be so," did not forbid secular government to his apostles and other disciples or condemn it as something evil was further demonstrated by the following: He forbade them to take either bread or money, bag or staff, or to have two coats apiece or shoes.[83] Who will say that he thereby wants to forbid the good created things that God gives to men for their benefit, especially because Mark says that Christ commanded them to carry nothing except a staff, and that they should wear sandals, etc. From this it is clear that his sole intention is that they perform the preaching office entrusted to them with the greatest diligence and not allow themselves to be distracted by anything they might require, not

---

[75] 1 Sam. 8.

[76] *Got fer[n war]*, literally: God was distant or remote.

[77] Deut. 17:14–20.

[78] 1 Sam. 8:11–18.

[79] Cf. Isa. 10:5.

[80] Job 34:30, Vulgate.

[81] Isa. 3:4.

[82] Hos. 13:9–11.

[83] Luke 9:3; Matt. 10:9–10; Mark 6:8–9.

even those things related to the needs of the body, and involve themselves in no other care for temporal things. For this reason he promised them what they would have need of. In the same way he forbade them the lordship of secular government as something of no use to the kingdom of God, faith, or love. He desires that the fire that he has ignited[84] should always burn without any hindrance.

And in order that this be better understood: by means of the gospel Christ has superseded the law, not that it should no longer exist or no longer be valid, but that it should be completely and fruitfully fulfilled in the spirit, and not in appearance only, as with hypocrites, and also that it should no longer frighten the conscience. Formerly it was nothing but letters in stone tablets; it only killed. Now it is pure spirit, for he writes it in the hearts of his believers, where it gives life. The letter kills but the spirit gives life.[85] It is all the same word of God, but the effects are different. In the Old Testament there was a preaching office that killed by the letter; in the New Testament there is a preaching office that gives life through the spirit. In the same way, secular government is not suspended by the gospel or the kingdom of Christ, so that it no longer exists, but only so that it not be exercised in a worldly way, with pomp, arrogance, suppression, but rather in a Christian or spiritual way in the service of the gospel or spiritual realm and that it minister to the eternal kingdom.

Therefore Christ excluded himself from the secular realm in so far as it is secular and not of benefit to the eternal, spiritual realm, but rather detrimental, as he said to Pilate: "My kingdom is not of this world."[86] That is to say: I do not rule in the worldly, heathen fashion of those who avenge themselves, tyrannically flaunt their power, and seek their own gain in secular matters, not asking about God, their neighbour, or eternal, spiritual good. Thus he himself proclaims: "If my kingdom were of this world, my servants would fight" to prevent me from suffering or being oppressed.[87] He does not deny that he rules in the world and over the world. For he says

---

[84] Cf. Luke 12:49.

[85] 2 Cor. 3:3, 6.

[86] John 18:36.

[87] Ibid.

himself: "All power has been given to me in heaven and on earth."[88] Thus the temporal government of the secular realm has also been given to him, so that at the end of this world he will deliver the kingdom to God the father and relinquish every rule, authority, and power. But meanwhile he must reign until he has put all his enemies under his feet.[89] For this reason David admonishes all kings and secular rulers to act in the fear of God and rejoice,[90] not with wanton pride but with trembling, and to be clever, wise, and disciplined or humble. But this happens when they kiss Christ the lord, the true son of God,[91] pay homage and allegiance to him, conduct their government according to his word, and faithfully promote his spiritual kingdom. Otherwise they will not escape the fearful wrath of God or damnation but perish along the way. We have a beautiful text for this in the Book of Wisdom [6:1–5]: "Listen therefore O kings, and understand; learn, O judges on earth. Give ear, you that rule over multitudes, that exalt yourselves above the clouds. For power was given you from the Lord and sovereignty from the Most High, who will search out your works and inquire into your plans. Because you are ministers of his kingdom" (for which reason you must serve the kingdom of God) "but do not rule rightly, or keep the law, or act according to the commands of God, he will come upon you terribly and swiftly, because severe judgment falls on those in high places. For the lowliest man will be pardoned but mighty men will be mightily punished and a severe judgment will befall the powerful." This applies to those who behave with force, are arrogant in their power, and do not faithfully and obediently serve the gospel of Christ. From all of this it is clear that secular rulers should and can use their office or sword in all matters which they can discern, regardless of whether those matters belong to the spiritual or corporeal kingdom, and they should conduct their office principally in the service of Christ and his gospel. But they must take care that they not seek their own good or, abandoning their office, usurp someone else's and under the appearance of protecting the gospel conceal their

---

[88] Matt. 28:18.

[89] 1 Cor. 15:24–25.

[90] Ps. 2:10–12.

[91] Ps. 2:12, ASV.

tyranny, as those do who have not yet learned what the gospel or kingdom of Christ is, much less have it in their hearts, who have never paid homage to Christ, but who simply fear to be robbed of their power, interfere blindly, and kill or execute for reasons of doctrine or faith, etc. Their power as such is good, but they do not serve Christ with it and do not seek the truth of the gospel but rather their own tyranny, and thus they act contrary to the kingdom of Christ, which is a kingdom of truth and justice. This is a damnable and harmful abuse. Nor are such murderous tyrants excused when they say that they do it out of good intentions toward the Christian church and fancy that they are thereby doing God a service.[92] For intentions and suppositions are no good here; certainty is required. A ruler must know for sure how or when he should use his power. Thus he should judge or rule solely according to God's word and be absolutely certain beforehand that what he wants to use his sword against is opposed to God and evil, and repugnant or harmful to the kingdom of God.

The Turks[93] also think that they are doing God a service when they persecute Christians; so do the papists when they exterminate Lutherans or others whom they denounce as heretics. Their priests and scholars talk them into it; but this does not excuse them, for they should use their sword not according to their own opinion or human teaching or regulations but only according to God's word and pleasure. Otherwise, they will err because they act apart from faith. "For what does not proceed from faith is sin."[94] If the government wishes to punish a deceptive, false teacher, it must be certain beforehand that he is such and acts contrary to God's kingdom. But if it wants to execute him, it would only be fair to be sure that he would remain obdurate and not repent. One must deal wisely and in the fear of God, not tyrannically.

SECOND. Now that we have shown how the spiritual and secular realms not only exist side by side but also that each assists the other with its office etc., we will now further demonstrate that one may and also in certain circumstances can administer the other's office and deal with matters pertaining to the other realm. As for

----

[92] John 16:2.
[93] On the following, cf. p. 45.
[94] Rom. 14:23.

example, when the secular government uses the sword or power it has received from God in spiritual matters, such as preaching, ceremonies, administration of the sacraments etc., or, on the other hand, when the spiritual government does the same thing with respect to secular affairs, temporal goods, court cases etc. This we know from scripture, for many kings are praised as godly because they repressed false doctrine and destroyed false worship with the sword or force[95] according to the law of God which commands that those who do such things be killed.[96] And if someone says that this is in the Old Testament and was the law of Moses,[97] it is easy to see that this comment is worthless, for the secular government has no less power in the New Testament than in the Old. In fact, it has much greater freedom to act and to use its power as love demands, without fear, because the New Testament is free and unfettered and permits free dealings to the extent of one's love for God and one's neighbour. But the Old Testament held people in fear, so that they had to act according to the precise goal or letter of the written law, and were not nearly so free to use their goods, talents, offices, and occupations as is now the case in the New Testament under grace, just as a child has more rights or freedom than a servant. And the heir, as long as he is still a child, is kept under discipline and not given as much freedom as when he comes of age and secures possession of his inheritance. Thus there need be no doubt that a secular government should also have power to act in spiritual matters, as they may be called, where, how, and to the extent that Christian love demands it for the betterment and furtherance of the spiritual realm, but by no means for its detriment or hindrance. For if the body helps the soul with its work, and a man helps God, why not also one government or regime the other, a prince an apostle? One must not attach too much importance to the details or the circumstances,[98] because it is certain that every-thing that happens out of Christian faith and love is wholesome

---

[95] For example: 1 Kings 15:11–13; 2 Kings 10:28–30, 18:1–8, 22:1–2, 23:4–25.

[96] Deut. 13:1–5.

[97] An opinion expressed by the anonymous Nürnberger; see p. 42.

[98] "Man darf nit die object oder umbstend hin und wider gross wegen." A more cautious translation would read: "One must not *consider too carefully* the details or the circumstances."

and good, since it is according to the teaching and command of Christ. Thus when a government enlightened by the spirit of true faith finds that a false doctrine is causing damage, or that certain abuses in divine worship need to be altered and good order established, and whatever similar cases there may be, the love of God and its neighbour compel it to take action. It cannot do so with preaching or in a spiritual manner, for it is perhaps not sufficiently learned to do so and has no call. Thus it follows that it must undertake the task with its sword and power according to the limits and measure of its calling. It must not wait for legates, prelates, or councils to accomplish this. For in general little trust is to be placed in such people. And would God that emperor and princes did not allow those consecrated idols[99] to intimidate them so[100] but rather vigorously used their offices now for the increase of Christ's kingdom, summoned councils, examined doctrines, protected truth, repressed falsehood, and ordered all things in the churches to the best advantage of the common welfare etc. If they did, the church would really be in better shape. But now the so-called spiritual estate does not do it and, for the sake of their own gain, only hinders others who could do so.

Let us assume that there were no bishop, preacher, or pastor in a given place, or that those who claimed to be such did not fulfil this pastoral office; should blasphemy, abuse of the gospel, seduction of the innocent, and other offences on that account be left unchecked? For God through Moses ordained government first of all,[101] and thereafter the law, divine worship, and priesthood, as the things according to which and on account of which the government should exercise its office. Since then he establishes no government except on the condition that it should serve his word and kingdom. For this reason authority or secular government is called God's ordinance and God's servant,[102] as something that should serve his word, will, gospel, or law. One may not say:

---

[99] *Ölgötzen* (literally: oil-idols), i.e., statues of saints before which oil lamps were hung. This image is here applied derisively to the Catholic clergy.

[100] A very free translation of a phrase that actually says "to cause [emperor and princes] to stare at them [the idols] with wide open mouths."

[101] Deut. 1:13–17.

[102] Rom. 13:1–4.

"Moses has nothing to do with us,"[103] for Christ himself says that Moses had written of him[104] and refers everyone to Moses as to a witness of the gospel, as Abraham too says in Luke 16[:29–31] that one should hear Moses and the prophets if one wishes to escape damnation. Why then should a government not use its sword according to Moses and the prophets?

For this reason no pious Christian should despise the examples in the Old Testament, which show how the pious fathers dealt according to God's law, in order to govern their conduct by it. Another reason is that examples of the heathen too are given to us in the gospel for our improvement and for imitation, such as the Ninevites and the Queen of Sheba,[105] Tyre and Sidon,[106] etc. Indeed, one should test all doctrines and spirits, as St. Paul says: "Test all things; hold fast to that which is good."[107] A Christian should accept whatever serves faith and love and conduct himself accordingly in his office or personal life. For St. Paul and the other apostles often dealt according to the law even though they were by no means bound to it in conscience.[108] And our beloved lord, Jesus Christ, bases the whole gospel on the law and the prophets, when he says: "Whatever you wish that men would do to you, do so to them: for this is the law and the prophets."[109] Again in Luke 10[:25–27], when the lawyer asked him, "What shall I do to inherit eternal life?" he answered: "What is written in the law? how do you read?" etc. In sum: to love God above all things and one's neighbour as one's self is the entire law and the prophets, etc. Thus, although the force of the law and the oracles of the prophets only lasted until the time of John the Baptist,[110] when Christ came, who through his flesh has abolished the law of commandments, in so far as they were written down and, like a partition wall, made

---

[103]As had Luther in his *Unterrichtung, wie sich die Christen in Mosen sollen schicken,* WA 16:373.3f and 21f. The anonymous memorandist made use of Luther's argument; see p. 42.

[104]John 5:46.

[105]Matt. 12:41–42; Luke 11:30–32.

[106]Luke 10:13–14.

[107]1 Thess. 5:21.

[108]For example, Acts 16:3.

[109]Matt. 7:12.

[110]Luke 16:16.

enmity between us and God,[111] and who fulfilled both the law and the prophets: he nevertheless confirmed and commanded the law to us, to conduct ourselves according to it as a rule, to the confirmation or strengthening of the gospel. Therefore a Christian magistrate may and should conduct his office according to the contents of the law and the prophets. Through faith the law is not abolished but rather upheld, Rom. 3[:19–31]. The law shows what one should do or not do; the gospel shows and teaches in what manner such works become right, good, and holy to the glory of God.

But since both law and gospel require that every individual should use his calling to the love of God and his neighbour, Christian love demands that a government, by its power or sword, should establish Christian doctrine as much as possible by appointing, training, and fostering true and qualified teachers, just as emperors and other secular governments have, according to ancient and praiseworthy custom, provided bishoprics and other churches with suitable persons, which right, and others as well, the pope has now thievishly usurped and reserved for himself. Why then should a government not also have the corresponding power, for the sake of its subjects' welfare, to restrain false teachers and banish false doctrine, and thus serve with its office the kingdom of Christ, to which doctrine chiefly belongs? *Illius est destituere, cuius est instituere.*[112] For every Christian is earnestly commanded to test all spirits and doctrines, to accept the wholesome and reject the harmful.[113] Why then should a government, as guardian of its subjects, not use its power to assure that true, saving doctrine be preached and damnable doctrine shunned? For divine scripture subjects all men without distinction to secular government. When St. Paul says "Let everyone be subject to the governing authorities,"[114] no one is exempted. If, then, every single person is subjected, how much more so that office, service and whatever anyone publicly and with everybody's knowledge does, has, or can

---

[111]Eph. 2:15–16.

[112]"Whose the right to appoint, his the right to dismiss." The source of this legal maxim has not been identified.

[113]1 John 4:1.

[114]Rom. 13:1.

accomplish for the sake of God. Pilate had power to judge Christ and his preaching office, but he had no power unjustly to condemn.[115] Thus every government has the power to punish evil works and reward good ones, to the extent that it can know either, for one must leave good or evil thoughts and desires to the judgment of God, who alone searches hearts and minds.[116]

Now no one can deny that preaching or teaching is an external work, true preaching a good work, false teaching an evil work. Thus one must concede that a government may punish such evil works and restrain those who use their preaching office improperly. One must only take care that the matter be thoroughly investigated and that one not condemn Jesus and free Barabbas.[117] One does not thereby interfere in God's kingdom or assume the right to rule over faith etc., but merely uses one's legitimate office for the service of Christ, faith, and the kingdom of God, just as when one punishes and restrains blasphemy, perjury, or other evil external works, to the glory of God, which is injured thereby. Even though government has as little authority over the glory of God as it does over God's word or faith, it nevertheless punishes what is contrary to God's glory, etc. Thus, although it cannot master the kingdom of God or destroy the kingdom of Satan, nevertheless it must use its office in the service of that end.

Concerning the other external ceremonies, there is no doubt that a government must regulate them, for they belong indisputably to the kingdom of the world and not to God's kingdom, for God's kingdom does not come with external gestures, and one cannot say, "Lo, here or there it is."[118] Therefore everything that occurs by means of observation or external gestures belongs to the secular realm, as does everything that has persons, time, place, and the like. One cannot say: The kingdom of God is at Rome, Jerusalem, with the pope, cardinals, bishops, councils, fathers, in these or those works, in this or that time, etc., for it is inward in the conscience, spirit, and truth.[119] Whatever is external, personal,

---

[115]Cf. John 19:10–11.

[116]Ps. 7:9; Jer. 11:20.

[117]Matt. 27:26.

[118]Luke 17:20–21.

[119]John 4:24.

temporal, must always belong to the secular, temporal realm. To the spiritual power Christ has promised that whatever they do on earth with respect to binding and loosing shall be eternally valid in heaven.[120] But the secular government is purely temporal. When he yields up the kingdom of God to the father,[121] Christ will abolish all lordship, government, and power, as things ordained to serve the kingdom of God for a time only. Just as many spiritual gifts, like prophecy, tongues, knowledge, and similar works, will cease when perfection comes, for God established and granted them to serve his kingdom for a time only. Thus the more spiritual a Christian becomes, the more he belongs to God's kingdom and is freed from the secular kingdom. But since no one can be completely spiritual in this mortal body and life, everyone must be subject to secular government, first because one is still carnal, and second, because one should lovingly serve others who are still carnal. The false, misleading teachers are completely carnal, brutish, material, without the spirit of God and understand nothing of that spirit.[122] Thus they do not belong to the kingdom of God, but rather to the world, and in so far as they teach falsely, they misuse the preaching office, from which they should for that reason be removed. Indeed, as far as they are concerned, they degrade themselves and yield themselves to the secular realm.

Just as a man can be both spiritual and carnal and under both the spiritual and the temporal kingdoms, so a Christian government with its office can be of service to the spiritual and the temporal kingdoms, as outlined above.[123] Nevertheless, in so far as a secular government deals with spiritual matters that serve the kingdom of God by means of commands or bans, punishments or rewards, this must all happen and be handled in such a manner that consciences remain unencumbered and God's kingdom unimpeded. For in the kingdom of God, to which all power is subject, the government is only a servant, and does not rule over faith, conscience, gospel, etc. Thus when it banishes false doctrine or forcibly defends true doctrine, it does so as a service, just as when one receives a prophet

---

[120]Matt. 18:18.
[121]1 Cor. 15:24.
[122]1 Cor. 2:14.
[123]See pp. 85ff.

in the name of a prophet.[124] That is to use power for service and to turn lordship into servitude, tyranny into government. Only Christians can do this, who turn greed into love, have wives as though they had none, weep as though they were not weeping, buy as though they would not keep it etc.,[125] are also preserved from sin only by such humility, do not use their government and secular power in worldly, tyrannical fashion, as arrogant lordship, but as God's ministers and the servants of their subjects; they know that their power and government is a human institution and creation instituted by God, wherefore they must be under and not over the kingdom of God, and not a ruler but a servant of God and his word, and use their entire office for such service, yet with such discernment that they are certain, without error or doubt, that they do right and serve God, and do not imagine on basis of doubtful illusion that they are doing God a service,[126] like those fools who forcibly protect or repress doctrines which they neither understand nor are certain whether they are true or false.

A servant of God or a Christian ruler must be faithful and wise[127] so that he can with certainty use his sword in God's service. One's complaint is not that kings or princes protect true doctrine with the sword and repress the false, but that they do it without discernment and irresponsibly, ignorantly condemning truth, and are more concerned about their own power than about God's kingdom, desiring to be lord of the world and not God's servant, doing evil in the hope of producing good,[128] venturing by means of a great evil to prevent a small one, as when[129] they compel the poor people to deny or confess their faith and to say things other than what are in their hearts (over which no secular government can have power); in this way they burden themselves with the lies and false confessions of such weak people. "Even if their subjects were in error, it would be much easier simply to let them err than

---

[124]Matt. 10:41.

[125]1 Cor. 7:29–30.

[126]John 16:2.

[127]Matt. 24:45–51.

[128]Rom. 3:8.

[129]The balance of this paragraph is a paraphrase, with some direct quotation, from the section of Luther's *On Secular Authority* found in AE 45:108–9.

to compel them to lie and to utter what is not in their hearts." That is to cure one evil with a worse one, to destroy a whole country in order to save one city.

Concerning this, David says in Psalm 2[:10]: "Be wise, O kings, and love righteousness, you who judge land and people."[130]

When a Christian ruler conducts himself faithfully and wisely in his office as a servant of God, this question and others like it will quickly be decided. May God grant his help. Amen.

Until wiser heads produce something better.[131] *Cum iudicio pio legendum.*[132]

---

[130]Cf. Wisd. 6:1.

[131]"Auf verbesserung baß verstendiger," a stock phrase in the bureaucratic language of the time. The full meaning is: "Until those with a superior understanding produce something better[, this is my opinion]."

[132]"To be read with pious judgment."